Praise for
Cultivating a Servant Heart

T0010403

"None of us is where we are today because we got here on our own. We have all had those around us help sometimes in unexpected, small but significant ways, while others may have had a larger imprint. Those who read [this] book will be more grateful for those who have positively shaped them in the past and be more purposeful in how they make a positive difference in the lives of those around them. God knows, the world needs more of that. This book is a must-read for all of us."

—**Chuck Wachendorfer**, President, Distribution, think2perform, and author of *Don't Wait for Someone Else to Fix It*

"Where else can you join this many meaningful conversations with servant leaders in one place? I couldn't put these transformational stories down!"

—**Misty Lown**, entrepreneur and author of *One Small Yes*

"Caitlin Wilson takes readers on their own inward journey into the center of leadership and service . . . the heart. Highly recommend this read that plants itself deep."

—**Tita Yutuc**, LCSW, LICSW, President/CEO, Family & Children's Center

"Through the stories of others, Caitlin Wilson has successfully captured the deep connection between servant leadership and spirituality, compassion, and growth mindset. Over chapters, we get to know the storytellers as if they are sitting in rocking chairs in our own family rooms, sharing their unique voices and experiences."

—**Perri Richman**, MSOP, Chief Marketing Officer and Principal, The Brand Promise

"Servant leadership feels massively important at this moment in history. But my understanding of what it means to be a 'servant leader' sometimes feels inspiringly simple, and other times, confusing and amorphous. The gift of this book is that it provides intimate new perspectives on the reality of servant leadership from real people working to embody it in their communities. The best way to learn a skill is to see it performed. This book does that."

—**George McGraw**, Founder and CEO, DigDeep, and Los Angeles Water and Power Commissioner

Cultivating
a
Servant
Heart

The Servant Leadership Series

*Building a community of readers
for the common good*

Series Editor: Dr. Richard Kyte, Director of the
D.B. Reinhart Institute for Ethics in Leadership and
Endowed Professor of Ethics at Viterbo University

What Is Servant Leadership?

Servant leadership stems from the conviction that the best leaders are those who have a deep personal commitment to the common good   that is, to the well-being of all and not just a few—and out of that commitment comes the desire to lead. What this means is that good leadership cannot be defined merely in terms of principles, techniques, or strategies; it is primarily a matter of character, originating in love and culminating in effective action. The foundational insight of servant leadership is that all leadership, properly understood, is an exercise of virtue and can be evaluated according to whether it leads to a flourishing life for individuals and communities. The practice of servant leadership seeks to inspire and engage people to work for the greater good every day.

The D.B Reinhart Institute for Ethics in Leadership

Since 1999, the D.B. Reinhart Institute for Ethics in Leadership at Viterbo University has brought people together in fruitful conversation about ethical ideas and issues, inspiring people to lead ethical lives while at the same time helping to develop leadership abilities to further the common good in communities and organizations.

Cultivating
a
Servant
Heart

Insights from Servant Leaders

Caitlin Mae Lyga Wilson

Fulcrum Publishing
Wheat Ridge, Colorado

Library of Congress Cataloging-in-Publication Data

Names: Wilson, Caitlin Mae Lyga, author.
Title: Cultivating a servant heart : insights from servant leaders /
  Caitlin Mae Lyga Wilson.
Description: Wheat Ridge, Colorado : Fulcrum Publishing, [2023] | Series:
  The servant leadership series | Includes bibliographical references.
Identifiers: LCCN 2023012565 (print) | LCCN 2023012566 (ebook) | ISBN
  9781682753750 (paperback) | ISBN 9781682753767 (ebook)
Subjects: LCSH: Servant leadership. | BISAC: BUSINESS & ECONOMICS /
  Leadership | BIOGRAPHY & AUTOBIOGRAPHY / Business
Classification: LCC HM1261 .W56 2023 (print) | LCC HM1261 (ebook) | DDC
  303.3/4--dc23/eng/20230404
LC record available at https://lccn.loc.gov/2023012565
LC ebook record available at https://lccn.loc.gov/2023012566

Cover design by Kateri Kramer

Unless otherwise noted, all websites cited were current as of the initial
edition of this book.

Printed in the United States
0 9 8 7 6 5 4 3 2 1

Fulcrum Publishing
3970 Youngfield Street, Wheat Ridge, Colorado 80033
(800) 992-2908 • (303) 277-1623
www.fulcrumbooks.com

For Eric

Contents

Foreword

Tom Thibodeau
Distinguished Professor of Servant Leadership,
Viterbo University

A Tribute to Storytellers and Story Listeners Everywhere

At a recent funeral of one of our students, he was honored by a high school friend who said, "Javon taught me that when a stranger comes into our lives and knocks on the door to our hearts, we must open the door, pull up a chair, and listen carefully."

Caitlin Wilson is a storyteller and a story listener. She has learned to open the door to her heart and listen carefully to the stories of others. She asks generative questions about service, leadership, mentors, role models, virtues, and human limitations. She

understands that all of servant leadership development is character development, which is learned
throughout a lifetime of sacrifice and significance.
All our lives are stories with beginnings and endings,
comedy and tragedy, triumph and darkness. Caitlin
reverently and intentionally lets the stories speak,
revealing the characters of those who have followed
the call to serve and lead. Leadership is who we are
and who we are becoming. Servant leadership is
to engage and inspire others to work for a Greater
Good every day. Caitlin's writings validate and affirm
the faithfulness to this call.

As you read this book and savor the stories, open
the door to your heart, pull up a chair, and listen carefully to your inner self who has a story to tell and is
yearning for a Caitlin Wilson to listen.

> **"Be aware, you never know when you are
> entertaining an angel."**
> —DOROTHY DAY

Opening

In this opening I offer what feels intuitive to share right now with you, beloved reader, as you hold the important question of how to cultivate a servant heart.

If we listen closely to fear, anger, and division that surrounds us, we may really hear we are living in a time of collective yearning for deep connection.

Indigenous author, teacher, and advisor Sherri Mitchell writes of the great difference in values between Euro-American societies and Indigenous Peoples. Our larger society has valued individuality, youth, competition, aggression, speaking, conquest, arrogance, saving, exclusivity, fragmentation, and winning. Traditional Native American values run in stark contrast: community, elders, cooperation, patience, listening, harmony, humility, sharing, inclusivity, wholeness, and collaboration.

One may look at our times and see an era where the greatest choice we can make is to reimagine what we value. A re-returning to precolonial, prepatriarchal society principles. Today's prophets are speaking ancient wisdom into modern life. They are pointing to what our elders taught us: We are living in a time of prophecy.[1]

We are beautifully complex humans, full of emotions, stories, hormones, and an overriding, intuitive capacity to love, should we choose it. Once we become aware, we can choose it; once we choose it, we continue to choose it; once we have ingrained it into our way of living, we can inspire others to live in this way; when we are inspiring one another, we tend our collective yearning.

To inspire a life of love over self is to be a servant leader. And now, we need awakened servant leaders to awaken the servant leader inside all of us more than ever—in all walks of life, all corners of the world, all dimensions of living.

There is something special about the heart of a person who lives her life this way.

The short novel *The Journey to the East*, written by Herman Hesse and published in 1932, inspired the life work of Robert Greenleaf, the founder of the modern servant leadership movement. Within its pages, Greenleaf saw our human dilemma: "Except as we venture to create, we cannot project ourselves beyond ourselves to serve and lead."[2]

One may claim Greenleaf dedicated himself to the questions, "What is servant leadership, and why servant leadership?"

The next question is, "How? How do we cultivate servant hearts?"

The inspiring insights and stories that follow were shared by servant leaders in the field. Humans who have made it their life work to serve in several different types of environments—schools, organizations, faith communities, city streets. They describe their childhoods, journeys, visions of the future, and passions—all of which continue to cultivate their servant hearts.

This is a book about how servant leaders have begun—and continue to—cultivate hearts to love. "Continue to" because the work of softening the heart is never done.

This book was the idea of my teachers and mentors, Dr. Rick Kyte, Tom Thibodeau, and Sam Scinta. It was their vision for a book of interviews with people practicing servant leadership in the field, organized by seven key questions, instead of topics. This instinctive, rather than premeditated, approach may be better suited to reveal truths to each of us, for it is through intentional action woven with contemplation and reflection that we best answer our own life questions.[3]

The people we chose to interview represent the diverse range of applications to which servant leadership can be applied. Our interviewees are not just working in business settings, but among those experiencing homelessness, as part of faith communities, in schools, and in families. The decision to expand beyond business and institutions was deliberate; servant leadership in this experience may be thought of more as a way to live one's life rather than a theory of management.

Kyte emphasizes, "Human Beings are storytelling creatures. We live not just in the present, but in the future and past as well, and our lives are interwoven into the lives of others: our real lives and our possible lives are interwoven with the real lives of others, and the threads weaving them together are named hope and regret."[4]

I wanted to go as deep as I could into each person's heart, so I structured our conversation around an arc of past, present, and future. Reflection in the past, intention in the present, aspiration in the future.

One of the more poignant moments of the interviews came when an interviewee told me he felt seconds away from transcendence at any given moment—and then our call disconnected. This was a message to me: focus on the inner life. The inward journey. A concept I have become passionate about through my own life experience.

Another particularly moving moment was a story another interviewee shared about a tree that saved his life. This first caught my attention (two months prior my son's life was saved by a tree—a lower branch slowed his fall from a higher branch enough that it softened the impact). He went on to put himself in the shoes of the tree, and its life purpose: to save him. His message, "Be the tree," left me with the questions: "Who was I born to save? And am I intentionally cultivating a heart, the inner conditions, to save?"

Orientation: Intention of the Work

In sifting through these interviews that illuminated the inner lives of servants—people who have cultivated the heart to save—I hope to provide you, my beloved reader, and all of us, collective wisdom that inspires us to embrace wherever it is we are on our inward journey toward service—and to continue it.

Vietnamese Buddhist monk and mindfulness teacher Thich Nhat Hanh wrote a book in 2014 called *How to Love*. It's a little manual of teachings on how to love other humans. I like to think of this book as How to Serve.

The reflections and stories come from people serving a wide variety of humans—humans who are experiencing homelessness, learning, working, addicted to substances, teaching. The insights can be applied anywhere.

If you are on a servant leadership journey and looking to deepen your experience and soften your heart, these insights are for you.

Interviews
with Servant Leaders

*Stories and Insights
from the Field*

PAST

Reflecting on Foundations of the Journey
(Where We Have Been)

Who were your earliest examples of leadership,
and how did they shape you?

If we were all born with a map that revealed itself to us as we travel through life, what map were you born with? We can look to our roots for clues. Whether predetermined, serendipitous, or something else entirely, our earliest teachers ingrain our neural pathways with memories and stories that shape our identities.

Sue Rieple Graf

I had what some people would have considered an unconventional childhood. My grandpa, Stanley Sims—my mom's dad—was my first leadership impression. He was administrator of Lutheran Hospital and retired just as I was going into middle school in 1971. My grandpa knew everybody in the hospital by name. The cleaning staff, the housekeeping staff, the nurses, the doctors.

I think a lot of leaders know their inner circle. They don't always know the people at the "bottom" really doing the work. They don't really get to know them, make a relationship with them, know enough to call them by name. My grandpa, I felt, valued everybody who contributed anything in the patient care circle. And those people who are sometimes overlooked, like your housekeeping at your hotel, your coffee maker. I think we don't recognize those people enough and thank them for what they do.

A lot of people over the years have told me, "Your grandpa always treated me like I was his equal." So I thought that was pretty cool. And my grandpa also had a vision to grow the hospital—he was a big-picture person. He looked at contingency plans when those weren't even a thing. In 1961, there was a major fire at Lutheran Hospital, and more than a hundred people were evacuated safely in fifteen minutes. Now in 1961, there were not cell phones. There were not a lot of different things. So that's always stood out to me as a major thing.

He always made time for his family and us. My brother and I lived with our grandparents quite a bit on and off because my mom was mentally ill, and he always made time for us. He showed little home movies. He taught us how to garden. He taught us how to play cribbage. He and I built the doghouse together. I mean, we just did a lot of things together considering he was someone who was kind of an important community leader and, of course, had a busy position as a head of a hospital. He made time for what really mattered. His values didn't change. Values, God, family, work—and kind of in that order. And he also lived his faith out. He was someone who was kind to other people and looked for ways to help.

He shaped me to recognize other people for who they are and get to know their names. Be appreciative for everything. He had a strong moral value and a strong moral compass that was instilled in me. As a teenager, I ran a little bit wild, but always the thought was in my mind about dishonoring my grandpa or disappointing him; more importantly: it kept me from doing really stupid things. Probably, in hindsight, kept me alive, really.

Regina Siegel

When I think of servant leadership, it was my whole upbringing coming from a farm family. My maternal grandparents were dairy farmers, so everything was about taking care of people, loving people, literally providing life, giving food, milk, and sustenance to their neighbors and the greater community. And they took that very seriously. I remember having chickens, cats, and various different animals. Grandpa always taught my uncles, aunts, and mom to see everyone as having life. So the cats, we're going to squirt them with some milk, and we're going to feed and take care of them. Grandma would never bring them in the house, but every living creature, whether it be a person, or a fur baby, all have life. And our sole purpose in life, for us that comes from a Christian background, is to take care of people, and to really live as Jesus would have, the closest to that as we can.

I also come from a very humble family, so I was even thinking about this: Grandma would probably be like, "What are you doing putting yourself in a book?" You know, she always kept it real. She was valedictorian of her class. And if I didn't have straight As, there were going to be talks. But she would often ask me—even more importantly than the grades or how I was—she would ask, "What have you done to help out the world?" Or, "What have you done in your neighborhood to make it better?" Or, "How are you treating your parents and your family?" And I truly admired my grandparents, still do to this day.

Randy Nelson

There were several K–12 teachers and coaches who had a positive impact on me. But the first would be my T-ball coach. During a summer ball game, I was hit in the mouth while trying to field a ground ball. It resulted in a bloody lip. And I remember my coach, who was also the umpire in the game, stopping the game to carry me off the field and to the hands of my parents.

While there was a lot of blood and drama at the time, he became such a powerful influence on me. As a teacher, he lived just ten houses down on the same street as me. He was also the varsity baseball coach, and it was my goal to play for him as my coach some-day, which *did* happen. The varsity baseball field was across the street from my home, and I remember during the summer months I'd just sit and watch for him to come to the field to prepare it for a game. I was out there in a heartbeat. I picked rocks from the infield grass. I raked the batter's box and helped him with the hose to wet it down. I held the twine so that he could create a straight foul line. And all during this time, he remained connected to me by modeling the process and conversing with me.

He was one of about a dozen teachers that I could mention in a similar way. By the end of fifth grade, I knew I wanted to become a teacher. I gravitated to them. My dad was a bar owner, and he really struggled with his own alcohol dependency; was in treatment maybe five times in his life. And so, I somehow gravitated to my teachers. They were really good role models for me. Teachers are the reason I became an educator. I still connect with my T-ball coach, as well as many other educators from my past who blazed a trail for me, supported me, and encouraged me in my journey.

Lynn Nelson

I grew up in a small community near La Crosse. I saw servant leadership modeled through teachers, community, church, and my family. I had many role models that did good things for the common good of all. Growing up, it was never, *What's in this for me*? Or *We take care of our own*. It was more of a feeling of we are all in this together, and we have to work together.

My parents especially modeled servant leadership throughout their lives by volunteering and helping others. My mother worked at a nursing home for more than forty years. One of my earliest childhood memories was to drive to my great-grandparents' home so she could provide personal care for them and clean up their house—this after a full day of work.

Even to this day, she inspires me to help others. She is active in a community clothing and food bank. She is part of a small group of ladies who come in at 5:30 a.m. to sort through all of the donations that have come in and prepare them for distribution in the community.

Mike Desmond

I look back to when I was in my thirties. I was self-centered, and most things were about my career or "What's in it for me?" The thing that began to change my mindset was Rotary Club. A good friend of mine invited me to a Rotary meeting, and now I've been a member of the Downtown Rotary Club for more than twenty years. It seems like my first year in the club, they needed a chair for Mobile Meals. And I thought, "I don't know where my niche was yet," and so I said, "I'll do it." I've been the chair of Mobile Meals for twenty-plus years. That led me to becoming very involved in Mobile Meals of La Crosse, eventually serving on their board.

At Rotary I began to see the value of service. "Service above self." I looked at some of the members that were in Downtown Rotary; people who were respected in the community; leaders. I began to see exactly what made them successful. It wasn't by any kind of controlling, "I'm the boss" mentality. It was listening, caring, and a desire to help those in need. I admired that.

Joe Gillice

My parents were sixteen and seventeen when they had me. They were married for two years and then divorced when I was two. I lived with my mother and stepfather until I was about eight in Pennsylvania and then decided around eight or nine to go live with my father in Florida.

He didn't graduate from high school. He dropped out early because he got married, had a son, and so had to work. He worked as a bricklayer. When he moved to Florida, he was a shop teacher for a high school. While he was a shop teacher, he would do odd jobs on the weekends, like building outdoor fireplaces for people to earn some extra money. Eventually, he became an administrator for technical programs for Broward

County, Florida, so an administrator position at the county level.

He also opened a small, retail hardware store. So he would do his day job, 8:00 to 5:00, and then at night during the week go to the hardware store for a couple of hours, and then on the weekends, Saturday and Sunday, work in the hardware store. I would go and work with him on the weekends at the hardware store. Then over the years as his job got busier and busier, he had to scale back a little bit during the week, but still worked weekends and then eventually closed the store on Sundays.

My father was definitely my first example of someone that I thought and still think is a great leader. He led by example in his work ethic. Just thinking back to how old he was when he had me, and when I lived with him, he was in his mid- to late twenties and early thirties. He worked hard, not having a formal education, not having graduated from high school, and ultimately what he was able to accomplish in his career. I can remember being in college and saying to him one day, "I hope that I'm as successful as you financially when I'm older."

He said to me, "I hope you are more successful than me in your personal life." Again, you don't really understand it at the time, but as I've gotten older and I've looked back on his life, what do I think he could have done better in his personal life? That's helped influence me in what I think is important to me and my family now that I'm in that position.

Jervie Windom

My servant leadership journey goes all the way back to my childhood, just simply because my mom and my grandmother were servant leaders. I didn't know that at the time, they were just Mom and Granny; but they just served people, and it was always a part of my life.

Some of my earliest memories are of my mom always cooking too much food, because I was her only child. She didn't know how to cook for two, so she would cook more food than we needed. She would often plate that food and make me take it to the corner, where the liquor store was. And there would be people out there struggling with alcoholism who would hang out there.

I wasn't allowed to call them bums or anything like that because my mom would smack me upside the head. She would always ask, "When they were your age, do you think that this is what they wanted?" When we saw people that were struggling with drug addiction or alcoholism or whatever the situation, she didn't want me to pick on them. She wanted me to have a sensitivity and to be able to see them as human beings and see their worth and their value as people. And that was very important to her. And she enforced that in our home.

So she would plate this food and told me to take it up there, and I really didn't want to do it because it kind of cramped my style. It's not "cool." We were in the projects in New York City, and it's not cool to walk through the projects with a plate of food to go feed the alcoholics on the corner. But those people, my mom knew them by name, they were very important to her and she didn't give me an option, she made me do that, and I had better like it, or pretend to like it. She wanted me to do it with the right attitude. And she was right. I got to know those guys, I got to know their names, and I got to hear their stories, and they cared for me.

One day I needed to cash a check from my summer job. My mom always told me not to go by myself, but being the brave only child that I was, I decided to go by myself, and there was someone following me. The person cornered me not far from our projects, which was actually visible from the corner store. And when those guys at the corner store saw me being cornered by this person that was going to rob me, they came running down the street, "Hey, leave him alone! That's Diane's son. Leave him alone!" And the guy that was going to rob me took off running. It was then that I realized why my mom could walk through the projects anytime day or night.

It was amazing the relationships that she had with people, so much so that whenever she would go on vacation, there would be people waiting for her to come back, literally waiting on her steps for her to come back. She just had a way with people. Those were my beginnings.

My grandmother was the same way. She lived in South Carolina. Eventually I ended up living there, moving down with my grandmother. And my grandmother always knew who was sick in the neighborhood, and she would make food for them and have me go and serve them, check on them, or clean up their yards. I grew up not just caring for people, but I grew up being taught to care about people, that people had worth and their stories mattered. That was important to my mother and my grandmother.

Dave Skogen

My father was my earliest example of servant leadership, but I didn't realize what I was learning until I was older. Dad was a very giving person. He didn't care who got credit for things. I didn't realize it then, of course, because I was only five years old. Dad came to work every day, and he worked his tail off. He was tough on salespeople but kind to customers. When the customer was wrong, he'd treat them like they were right. Dad understood that our "Higher Purpose" is to serve and enrich the lives of others—most certainly the less fortunate. He did this on his milk route, and he did it as a grocer.

You can't really know what you want to do in life by just thinking about it—you have to do it and see how it fits. Therefore, I had a feeling early on as to how grocery might be a good fit, and how important giving back is. Unknowingly, Dad was telling my two brothers and me that "We are here to serve, not be served."

The truth is, there is only one profession, one calling, and that is: to Serve God by Serving Others.

Carolyn Colleen

In my early years, the leader that I looked up to, interestingly, was Whitney Houston. She's not a corporate leader, not a leader in any sense of what we would consider entrepreneurialism. But she was an artist. The reason I looked up to her is because she gave me a feeling of hope and inspiration in some of the darkest spaces of my life. I didn't have access per se to people in my world that gave me that hope. But when I would listen to her music, she gave me inspiration and hope that things would and could be better.

In one of her songs, she sings that they can take everything away from you, but they can't take away your dignity. And, in those words, and as those words rang, emerged a love—for no matter what happens, it's going to be okay.

She's someone I studied intensely, and she had a very rough upbringing, similar to mine. What she made out of it was finding her gifts in which to share with the world. And, even though her personal life was tumultuous, she was able to give the world her gifts, provide hope and inspiration, and uplift people with her art.

Whitney made me think, "Well, if she can do it, I should be able to do it too." Because she isn't perfect, she had hard times and still struggled through hard times throughout her life. But, despite that she still shined through the gifts, because in every bad there's still something good that could be found.

And she's someone I don't know. That's the thing that I feel is very important to point out, as humans, as we're curating what I call a board of directors. Businesses have a board of directors, nonprofits have a board of directors. Why wouldn't we, as humans, have our own board of directors? Who's in charge of your spirituality? Who's in charge of your finances, your relationships, your wellness? Who do you have in your personal life, on your personal board of directors?

Whitney was the first light. She was the first hope that spoke to me and said, "Hey, you know what? You might have something really special about you. How do you show it through, despite your adversity?"

Brian Haefs

When I was in high school, I was an athlete and wanted to play football. There were three grades in my school: sophomore, junior, and senior. And there were roughly five hundred to six hundred per class. It was a big school. They only played the juniors and the seniors for football. My goal was when I was a junior I wanted to start. I wanted to letter. And I did. I played on the offensive line. My coach, Sam, was hard on me, but there were only four juniors that started, and I was one of them. I worked hard, lifted weights, and always hustled. And the coach ended up making me a captain. It was really weird because usually it's the quarterback or running back, and I was on offense, and it was myself and another guy on defense, a defensive back. And I think what the coach was doing, looking back on it now, is that I blocked for people and served. So by serving, he gave me one of the leadership roles.

I went to see him when I was about thirty. He was the principal of the school. I said, "Hey, Coach, I understand you're retiring. Congratulations." He said, "Well, we got some bad news." I said, "Well, what's going on? Your health?" "No, not mine. My wife. She's got cancer, and I want to retire and spend time with her, all the time we can."

"I get it, makes sense." I said, "Hey Coach, just so you know, I had cancer."

He was Italian, a really emotional guy. He started tearing up. He said, "What kind of God would give you cancer?"

And I said, "Coach, it's okay. It's what I needed." I said, "I was a very proud person, I was mean, I used power. Now, I appreciate every day. I look for sunsets."

Sam helped me become a servant leader, and actually, part of it was my mother. I found out this later, but Sam would be real hard on me and yell a lot during the games when I was a junior. And it was the fourth game or fifth game, he just took me aside and we talked about what was going on; no more yelling.

I found out years later she had called the coach, made an appointment to see him, and said, "You can do whatever you want to, you're the coach. But I don't know if you're communicating with Brian in the best fashion." She said, "If you're yelling at him, he's probably not going to listen to the extent if you just pull him aside and talk to him." And he started doing that. So it wasn't just Sam. My mother understood how I operated, and part of servant leadership is to understand what makes people tick. Through that, my mother helped the coach grow also.

Aaron Rasch

The earliest person with the greatest impact on me was a man named Bubba.

Prior to meeting him, I was warned that he would likely swing at me. Bubba was in his mid-sixties, with some physical disabilities and an unsteady gait. I was told it'd be easy to get out of the way. I was twenty-one and starting a new job as a caregiver. Bubba would be my first client. His life was rough, spent mostly in mental institutions. There were stories of mistreatment, restraints, and isolation, especially when he was young. I was curious about his past but was told very little. He was considered "non-verbal," able to understand speech but only able to respond with sounds or parts of words.

Not having much to go from, my first days with Bubba were stressful. I'd help get him up from his chair and he'd try to scratch or bite me. While in the bathroom, he'd lunge and swing at me. He'd throw dishes at me and yell. I felt useless. When I asked for support or suggestions, I was directed to fill out an incident report, and encouraged to not take it personally. While looking in the file cabinet, I noticed he had a guardian, his sister Shirley. I decided to reach out to her with questions on how to help support her brother.

Fortunately, Shirley was very supportive of her brother. She lived five states away but was eager to offer stories of a gentler, kind person. She explained outings they'd do together—boat trips, visits with family, football games . . . . Shirley painted a picture of a joyful relationship with her brother. She offered to talk on the phone anytime. When I returned to work with Bubba, I told him about my conversations. I told him stories of boat rides and Green Bay Packers' games, and his eyes lit up with excitement. I continued talking with Shirley, and included Bubba too. He laughed and his sister helped me understand what Bubba meant to say. It took less than a week and Bubba's incidents became fewer and fewer. From four to five per day to once every couple weeks. It became clear that being understood was something important to Bubba, but not a task expected from caregivers. Listening to Bubba's deeper story gave insight into what every human wants, to feel understood and connected to people we care about.

Working with Bubba sparked a revelation in my heart. What if all human services engaged people with the same curiosity, intent, and compassion as my brief glimpse with Bubba. Perhaps people wouldn't be burned out from sacrificing so much time and effort on fixing, but more meaningfully listening and reinvigorating their own heart. The lessons learned from Bubba hold true to this day. Walking into tough moments is still challenging. I've taken some figurative "hits" along the way and can become frustrated by "impossible" situations. However, a slight perspective shift offers a sense of peace . . . to pause, seek to understand, and listen for the deeper story.

These early stories with Bubba were little sparks that showed me that there's a better way to live and connect with each other through life and work and to not be shy about it, to really put forth those values first, because that's a human condition that we're all kind of drawn into.

FUTURE
Creating Our Aspirations of the Horizon
(Where We Are Going)

What mission do you believe our era was uniquely called to carry out?

Similar to the map we were each born with, where are we on the map of humanity? Or as philosopher Grace Lee Boggs famously asked, "What time is it on the clock of the world?"[5] It's there, when paired with a vivid vision of what's possible, that our era's work awaits.

> **"Somebody needs to paint the big dream, to give our age a goal that will lift the eyes of young people off the ground and make them want to stretch their horizons."**
>
> —ROBERT GREENLEAF[6]

Sue Rieple Graf

We need to be mentors to younger leaders, modeling compassion and patience, and then you guys are
going to have to come up with the ideas. Bridging
the deep divide that exists currently between human
beings that aren't willing to sit down and really listen to each other and try to understand. They just
want to promote their agenda, whether it's political
or religious. I think our mission would be to work
at coming together to solve our world's problems,
our country's problems, our city's problems, and our
neighborhood's problems. Finding ways to bring
people together rather than throwing stones at the
other side.

I think it starts one on one. One on one and
trying to find political leaders that are going in
that direction rather than trying to divide. We can't
change the world. You and I aren't going to wake up
someday and change the world or the country or
even our city, but if we can, one person at a time, be
kind, show compassion, show empathy, try to understand the other person's point of view. Be patient

with each other, for Pete's sake. I think that people have become insanely impatient with each other.

Always assume that whoever you're talking to is doing the best they can. There was a woman yesterday at the hotel who showed up there and said, "I'm homeless. I need a space. I've been at Houska Park all summer." But why did she just show up yesterday? I don't know the backstory. She was demanding a room and there were no rooms. I mean, there was no way for us to help her. We let her vent. We listened to her compassionately. We agreed, "Yes, that would be very frustrating."

I think just how we treat people, consistently, all the time, whether we're at a coffee shop waiting for our order, at the bank behind a long line and we're frustrated. If we can try to understand the other person's point of view.

And you might not reach an agreement, but I think there are ways to be respectful to each other and compassionate and empathetic without necessarily agreeing on who the best president is or which religion is right. It's something that we have to practice until we become good at it, because the we-want-it-now mentality has brainwashed us into thinking that's how we should operate, so when we don't get what we want right now, and how we want it, we tend to lash out rather than try to work at how can we solve it.

Regina Siegel

I think we've been charged with bringing humanity back. Finding how we can focus on connection versus disconnect.

I feel like our era right now is charged with getting beyond what we've created—social media, schedules, all of the things that we've done that maybe aren't that important—and really finding connection, getting to know each other and having a safe planet. I would love it if everyone had adequate food, felt safe in their neighborhoods, and felt loved.

Can you imagine if we had the most simple and basic of human needs? If we had food, clothing, shelter. If we were safe, no matter where we slept, went to the store, drove, rode our bike, and that we knew someone cared about us. If every person had that, I think it would be a whole different world.

Randy Nelson

I think we are living (hopefully for the last time) through a time period where what it's like to be human is being seen through self-righteous eyes. People are finding the need to separate themselves from others through amplifying differences so that they can find the self-esteem necessary to please themselves or others who think like them or look like them. I believe we are here right now to reset our lives by first seeing each other as humans, and it is that collective bond that holds us all together. When we first understand that, we can solve any problem together. But when we cannot first accept ourselves as human beings, we will eventually allow the differences to be so magnified that we will destroy ourselves in some way.

I think we're in this time of binary thinking, that everything is black and white, and there's no gray. When indeed, where there are human beings, and the imperfections that come with human beings, there's gray. And I think that what's most important out in front of us here, is that the people who see and accept the gray can sometimes lead best. Because if that's not what happens, then we're leading through the binaries, and that's going to do more to separate us, and to amplify what's different about people, instead of what's the same about people. We're human beings. And I think we have a lot of work to do with our institutions, to better understand how our institutions actually serve more to sort people and separate people on differences, rather than to bring them together as human beings.

And I think the turbulence that we're all feeling right now is just that. You can't be in the middle. It's a dangerous path for us right now. I think that we have to accept the grayness, and we have to be able to navigate through the grayness. As human beings, we're not widgets. And every person has gifts, every person has foibles, and we need to support people in their journeys.

Lynn Nelson

We are living in some crazy times. I feel like beliefs and lifestyles have had a major shift to "What's in it for me—I take care of my own—it's my way or the highway." It's not going to be like turning a car around in a roundabout. This is going to be like turning a major ship around in troubled seas. It's going to take a long slow turn. But the turn can happen. We need to turn the ship around to more grounded living. Faith, common good, care for one another, and stepping out and leading. Encouraging and bringing people together.

Mike Desmond

Watching young people today, social media is becoming harmful. It allows people to say anything they want without being face-to-face with somebody. We've become a culture where you can take shots at people from a distance. To me, that's really wrong and creates a culture of insensitivity. We don't seem to solve problems face-to-face anymore, in talking with people, and getting to know the person. People need interaction with people. I think young people are going to lose social interaction skills. Interpersonal relationships are the key to good health, and creating a world of compassion.

I don't know how we get rid of the judgmental part of our society. This is the worst time in politics I've seen in my lifetime. They're not problem solvers. They attack the opponent. Is that going to become the way of life? I know from my own experience, the only way to get something done of any value is to collaborate with people, and people that don't agree with your point of view. That's okay and healthy. But we're living in a world now—and I think politics is a big driver of this—that "if you don't think like what I think, I viciously attack you."

It seems like it is becoming part of our culture; a culture of judgment instead of compassion. To take something like homelessness and turn it into a political issue. They take everything and turn it into a political issue. It's easy for people to be very judgmental about the homeless, or the mentally ill, or the criminal. Instead of attacking them, why don't we try to help them? I was a member of the La Crosse County Criminal Justice Management Council. One of the programs created was that we met with some of the major employers in town. We asked, "What would it take for you to hire somebody coming out of jail?" and they told us. So, we created a program through Western Technical College where inmates that are released from jail could go through a jobs program and at least get an interview. If you don't help, they're coming right back. Every bit of research tells you that they're coming back. So, wouldn't it make more sense to help these people? The jail right now is well over 50 percent full of people with mental health issues. Upon their release, if you haven't done anything to solve the real problem, which is their mental health, they will be offending again.

From a societal point of view, a divisive and judgmental culture destroys a culture of compassion and service to others.

When I was at the Boys & Girls Club, I saw so many good kids who had just been traumatized, abused, and abandoned as children. They needed mental health services. What I learned is, if you call it therapy, they'll resist it. So, we started a mental health program in partnership with Mayo Behavioral Health. We hired a therapist to come in the club as a staff member. She interacted with our members, playing basketball, cards, or other activities. The result was kids trickling into her office and talking. It was all accomplished through meaningful interactions.

I was also on a Heroin Task Force and we invited a couple of recovering addicts. Both of them said their drug use started when they were twelve to thirteen years old. They were very lonely and started using pot and things escalated. One girl said, "If you would've told me, I'll stick a needle in my arm, I would've bet you a million dollars I wouldn't have. I can't even get a shot (at the doctor). But I was so desperate . . . " Their drug use was triggered by loneliness and depression.

Joe Gillice

When you look back through history, they talk about the greatest generation and the one that went through World War II. When you look back at the seventies and some of the civil rights movement, it's easy to say, boy, those generations were meant to carry the torch or mantle for those specific events in time, right? Trying to apply that right now, boy, I have a hard time with it. Maybe give me fifty or seventy-five years and I can tell you.

It's easy to point to some problems, it's hard to say we're going to be able to figure them out. The political divisiveness in this country is out of control. It's hard to get anything done when folks can't compromise and come together. I think a lot of things fall under that political divisiveness issue. So you sit there and you watch the news, and whether it's a white cop on trial and then they may be acquitted or they may be found guilty and just the reaction between racial groups within the country.

I'd like to see us come together and unite around what's fair and what's legal, as opposed to, did this particular demographic come out ahead or behind on this particular decision? I may not be the most articulate when it comes to those issues, but again, I think it falls under the divide that we have in the country and can we bridge the gap politically, racially, economically? I don't know if we're in a position to do that, but I think the gap in those three areas is something that we need to figure out.

I feel like the political, racial, and economic environment is that one side has to win and one side has to lose. Under that scenario, there's not a lot of trust amongst the sides and the divisions. Building trust is important in the business world and any organization that you're trying to build.

I think that same principle would probably hold true politically, racially, and economically and to decide to trust each other that we're trying to accomplish something that's in all of our best interests and one side doesn't have to lose. Can we find a scenario where all the sides win? I don't know how we get there because even internally when we've hired new folks and brought them in and I go through what's important to me and how important the people are and what our values are, I've had someone come back to me six months later and say, "I didn't necessarily believe you when you first said it."

What they didn't say was, "It's taken me time to see you in action for me to believe it." Look, everyone's different, and maybe they were just a little bit more skeptical, or I didn't do a good job articulating it. That same would have to happen for us to solve these major problems in our era and does each side believe and trust in the other side?

Jervie Windom

I think it's the problem that has existed throughout the ages. It's really this idea of surrender. And here's why I say that, because in order for me to see people the way that God sees people, then I have to decide that God is right, even if that means that I'm wrong. I have to decide that, because a lot of times, even when we talk about justice, somehow we read the Bible or see how Jesus responded in situations and say, "Well, that's how it was *back then*." And not, "That's the right way to respond *through all times*."

Love is never old. God's right. And if you don't buy into love, then you've got to accept that you're wrong. Love is right. Grace is right. Kindness is right.

When Paul talks about, in Ephesians, "walking in the spirit," he says if we do that, then we won't fulfill the less of the flesh. The reason that we fulfill the less of the flesh, is because we don't want to walk in the spirit, because we don't see that these things are right.

Let's say you have a relationship with someone, your relationship with that person is not about right or wrong in the sense of whether their opinions are right or your opinions are wrong, it's really not about that. The right or wrong is whether or not I'm seeing that person as God sees them, *that's* the right or wrong.

Jesus, when he was with his disciples, most of the time they had no idea what he was doing and no idea what he was even talking about. And other people around him, Pharisees and the Sadducees; in Matthew chapter nine, he's eating with the task collectors. They asked, "Why are you hanging out with sinners?" It's because Jesus had a different lens. He saw that every single human heart mattered to him, they all had value, they all had worth, they all mattered. So if we agreed with that, then the whole world would be different. That's the problem throughout all time. Do we agree with him? Do we agree with love? Do we agree with kindness? Do we agree with gentleness? Do we agree with forgiveness? Do we agree with mercy? Do we agree with God? Have we surrendered to his way or is it our way? Is he right or are we right?

Because the truth is, if he's right, then all the things that really matter to us probably are nowhere near as important as we think they are at this moment. So somebody cut you off in traffic and you say, "Well, God is right. I should show mercy." You may pray for that person because you don't know what's going on with them. You don't know what kind of day they've had. You just hope to God that they're okay. You see how that's different, but it doesn't feel right. It feels like justice didn't take place and you need to say something to them or scream something. Well, is God right? Is mercy right? Is grace right? Is justice right? Is truth right?

And then even truth. We want to apply truth oftentimes to the things that we don't even know about. What I mean by that is—and I think that's always been the issue—truth is what God thinks about everything. *That's truth.* In my view, the simplest definition of truth is, what does God think about everything? *That's truth.*

These three things we say in our church a lot: you have to discover what God has to say about everything. You've got to decide that he's right, even if it means that you're wrong. Discover, decide, and then you have to depend on him solely to give you the strength to do the things that he says are right. So discover, decide, depend.

I think that's always been the problem. Us not seeing things the way God sees things. If we saw one another with the love, with the compassion, with the mercy of our Lord, I don't care what time or season, you can go back to the Dark Ages, you can go to the future, it does not matter, the world would be different. So we have to begin to see one another as God sees us. People matter to God, and because every human heart is so special to him, why aren't we more fearful when we treat one another badly? When we disrespect one another, when we're not kind, why are we not more concerned about that? We're more concerned about what people did to us than what we're doing to them. I can't fix what they do to me, but I answer to God for what I do to them. I never answer to God for how people treat me. I only answer to God for how I treat people.

Dave Skogen

The developing of character traits—humility being most important. Seventeen schools in this area have an elective course we call "Character Lives." And it's working. Test scores are not enough. We know we need to teach character, and help our students get these habits into their game. The Character Lives program teaches values through a proven servant leadership curriculum. When students learn the value of kindness, service, and empathy, they don't just walk out of school being competent at math and science. They walk away being capable, compassionate people—the future leaders of our community and our businesses. They understand that to lead is to serve.

Character is our moral maturity. It's knowing who you are and being guided by a clear sense of right and wrong.

Carolyn Colleen

In order for humanity to thrive, we need to be able to look back at our history. We can look back at our history to understand where we're headed. We can solve a lot of challenges. I think that what happens is we forget. And so going back, seeing what has been done, and then being in that present space to appreciate what has been done in order to add innovation as we move forward.

Where we are right now, there are beautiful lessons to be learned. We have the opportunity to create a world that has cultivated all kinds of solutions in solving world peace and hunger. We have more than enough resources to do so. So how do we, as a human race, come together to offer up solutions that are seated from what we already know?

So what happens in individuals, in communities, and in our world, is that we kind of rush past seeing those clues, because success leaves clues. Being able to see where we've been successful in the past, in which to set us ourselves up for success into the future, is vital.

The challenge is we have not come together to see that we already have the tools to fix some of the world's largest issues, in a bit more of equanimity in order to actually think and process information. So, in that space, when we add equanimity to the equation, along with seeing the clues that we already have, we already have tools and resources in which to solve some of the most major problems. Take space for the equanimity to honor what we already know and see that success leaves clues to create and solve our current and future issues.

Brian Haefs

Our greatest challenge is to bring people together for the greater good and to find common ground. Right now we're so divided as a nation, as a world, and it scares me. It's unfortunate when we can't disagree, but still respect each other's opinion and find a place where we can live together. It seems like that's gone away for some reason.

I believe it's about relationships. At first I thought it's listening. And listening is important for a servant leader. Don't get me wrong. But I think that comes later. I think it starts with making ourselves vulnerable, because then we're human, and that's something that everyone relates to. A lot of times leaders are afraid to make mistakes. And that's part of the disconnect. Vulnerable and genuine.

Looking back, I think I started to make myself more vulnerable when I was at Trane Company, when I would talk about some of the concepts in servant leadership. It's interesting because right before Christmas, during one of the meetings I had, I started talking about love. I was talking to a bunch of macho welders. I started talking about love and asked them to think about that. The next day we went into what that was. It's not a feeling, it's an action. This one guy, he was retired out of the service and was a Master Sergeant. I'm walking down one of the aisles and he's up on top of one of the HVAC units we were welding. From fifteen feet up in the air working, he goes, "Hey Brian, I've got something to say to you."

And I thought, "Oh boy, here we go." So I went around the back. He came down. We're standing behind this unit, so we're kind of by ourselves and people can't see that we're talking. And I thought, "Well, he's just going to blast me." And goes, "What you're saying is right." I asked him what he meant, and he said, "Well, let me tell you a story. My daughter is in choir, she's a junior. And they had to go sing down at the Rotary Lights. She left with her friends and went to see Santa, and he asked her what she wanted for Christmas. And she said, 'Three years ago, my cousin was killed in a gun accident. And he had given me a Christmas necklace that lights up, and I've lost it.'

"And he said 'Okay,' and they went back to sing some more. And then when they were done, there was a guy that caught her eye and said, 'Santa wants to see you, when you get a second.' So she went back to see Santa, and when she got there, he had a necklace that lit up." And this guy is telling me this story, and he starts crying. And it's just amazing how that works. I thought I was going to get my butt chewed, but here he tells me this heartfelt story. And he said, "That's what life's about. It's giving people what they really need."

Aaron Rasch

Some of these deeper disconnections are what are plaguing us, because we don't have these natural touch points to each other as much as we have in the past. How can we reintroduce those connections to kids? It'll be incredibly rewarding.

The lost connection to nature, which Richard Louv in *The Last Child in the Woods: The Nature Principle*[7] speaks about, how kids are getting more drawn into screens and lessons of nature—how we can bring that connection to each other through meaningful ways that we are coming together with a sense of shared purpose.

We have all the little adages and how it takes a village to really see opportunities and embrace them and to open up all the different levels of connection. They're there. We have to pay attention to it more. We sometimes tighten up. And for whatever reason, perhaps we don't want to be a burden on anybody. But we tend to not reach out for these opportunities to cooperate together.

If we stop looking at ways to care for each other outside this idea of services. It feels depressing to think that we have to rely on paid services for our parents when they get older or that we can't naturally incorporate them in some way in our lives. Those are questions we have to be open to address.

When I look at homelessness, when I look at loneliness, it becomes such a confounding concept to me. When you take La Crosse, we have probably 180 people, 200 people who are homeless at any given moment. And then, you look at people who have too much house to live in or this concept of people who are older adults who maybe need a little assistance from someone who's younger. And someone who's younger could use a little bit of purpose in their life to help somebody. Maybe we could share the housing. We have enough abundance to fit the needs of all our challenges. I just think we're not creatively connecting with each other enough.

How do we nurture the next generation?

Just as our earliest teachers planted seeds we now nurture, we are seed planters to others. How are we carrying our torch today in a way that best sets up those behind us to go further?

Sue Rieple Graf

We need to be mentors to younger leaders, modeling compassion and patience, and you guys are going to have to come up with the ideas. Somebody put on Facebook one day, "What's something that's not taught in schools that should be?" And people said things like that. Compassion. Empathy. I'm not sure how you could teach it except to model it. I can't tell someone to feel deeply in their heart for someone else's pain, I can only have them follow me and listen to me and watch how I treat people, or they have someone who has modeled it by caring for them.

Regina Siegel

Understand the enormity of our actions. Everything is leading by example and being in education, kids don't really just listen to talk or what you write. We need to understand that. The young professionals here at Trust Point, they're not going to believe something just because it's written down. They want to see it in action, they want to know that it's true.

So showing, getting to know our neighbors, holding the doors open, doing the things that are so essential to being kind. First treating each other with kindness and compassion, demonstrating that. And once we have that on a foundation, really feeding that curiosity. There are so many things to be discovered that we don't even know. The adults don't have all the answers. Those with one or more gray hairs as I do, we don't know, we don't know everything. But we really need to nurture the future and guide them and direct them away from strife and war and hatred and toward peace and love and caring.

I feel like they'll just take it off from there. Our parents, the leaders, need to lead with dignity and respect, and we need to echo that in our homes. We need to do that in our communities and pave the way for greatness ahead. I was lucky to have grandparents who were raised by their parents and their parents to be incredible leaders for me. We need to keep multiplying that. Then if you find someone who doesn't have that, if they have hatred in their heart or they don't know, we need to understand, not judge, and just see if they'd like some help. Invite them to dinner or to the grocery store with you when you're going, because you just don't know what people are dealing with.

Randy Nelson

We must encourage our next generation of learners to lead in ways that first seek to protect and support people. We must recognize and positively acknowledge individuals when they make ethical decisions that support people. We must model positivity. For the past several decades, we have allowed results and data to drive our decision-making to the point that people are sometimes not considered in decisions. Moreover, we have created deficit-thinking in just about every sector of our society. Wherever we have allowed experts to "set a standard" we have subsequently developed haves and have-nots, and those who are have-nots are labeled as inferior and need to be "fixed."

Leadership doesn't always have to be in charge of something. You don't have to be the person that's the flag bearer. Servant leadership to me can be a one-to-one conversation with someone. And no one even knows the conversation happened. I look at those people who have supported me along the way. I would've never made anything of those conversations that we had. But in retrospect, I do now. I think, "Wow, that changed my trajectory right there. And I didn't even know it at the time." And so those people may not see themselves as servant leaders as well, but indeed they are. And so you don't need to be the public face of something to serve others. You just do it.

Lynn Nelson

Being available to these new leaders. Continue to role model servant leadership. Start with oneself and continue to bring people into the circle. Encourage all your friends, family, and others to participate in five ways to give back throughout the year. You donate your time, you work with a group, you experience something that helps people realize that it's more than about ourselves; it's about us together. People have to experience that feeling of doing something for others, for no other reason than the good of the whole.

I found that with the elementary students I taught, too. Putting them in charge of things, even as fourth and fifth graders, saying, "We need to get this done." I would be busy and I'd look at a kid and say, "Can you organize this for me, right here?" And their chest would just pump up, and they would get the job done. As an elementary school educator, I was committed to giving students opportunities for leadership.

Mike Desmond

We create a culture of kindness and compassion, where judgment and hatred are unacceptable. Obviously, that needs to start as children at home and taught and reinforced in schools. We create a culture of service to others by providing opportunities to serve. We learn that the very best way to build a person's feeling of self-worth is to serve others.

Joe Gillice

We have about 150 people currently that work with us at our company. Those are the people that I can work with, develop, mentor, and maybe even inspire. The way you go about it, I believe, is one. It's important to communicate the values that you have as a person— professionally what's important to you—because those are what help drive your decision-making. When you're in a position of, well, I may have two or three alternatives, what's the best path?

Go back to your values and which one of those alternatives most closely aligns to your values. That's the right decision to make. For example, one of the values that we have is to do the right thing. If paying the sales team their commission because of an experiment that you ran cost them $10,000, pay them the $10,000. That's doing the right thing. That's an easy decision to make because of your values. Helping the future leaders with what your values are and helping them develop their own values is one way to help nurture the next generation of leaders.

Something that you do with kids, is you let them take risks and give them boundaries to work within to make their own decisions to help them grow. Same thing in your professional life. Future leaders and managers that you have, make sure they understand your values and what's important to you. Let them make decisions that are relatively low risk, they're not going to completely destroy the company if something goes wrong.

There are plenty of times I've said to folks, "Look, I don't agree with this path that you want to go down, but give it a try and see what you learn." I think that helps nurture and grow the next generation.

Jervie Windom

It starts with us receiving it for ourselves. There's a scripture where Paul talks about "grace abounding in us to every good work." I don't think we're able to write checks where there's been no deposit. Sometimes we try to convince people of things that we don't even possess ourselves, and it's not believable and it's not inspiring. Paul talks about, "What I'm giving to you is what was given to me." Paul had to receive so that he could give. At our church, at Resonate, we always say, "Stay inspired." We tell people that every single day, "Stay inspired."

Paul tells Timothy that it's inspired by God, but meaning "God breathe." And so, what's it like for God to breathe on you, and also to breathe in you every day? And then, when you breathe out, what you're giving other people is the breath of God that you received, as he breathed in. So literally you're just giving them what God has given you. That's the cycle of inspiration; first I have to receive it in order to give it to you. That comes with rest, it comes with us learning. As Peter Scazzero said, learning how to be human beings instead of human doings. What is it to just be and to know that is enough? God will never love you any more than he loves you right now. "Yeah, but what if I get this? And what if I accomplish this?" That's great. Kudos to you. But he will never love you any more than he loves you right now.

Dave Skogen

1. We have mandatory character classes in schools, like the Character Lives program. It's working. Test scores are not enough—we need to invest in the character development of young people. I

would sooner have my child get an A in leadership development than science.

2. Teach the value of money and how it relates to happiness. The recipe for happiness is to have just enough money to pay the monthly bills you acquire, a little surplus to give you confidence, a little too much work each day, enthusiasm for your work, a substantial share of good health, a couple of real friends, and a spouse and children to share life's beauty with you.

Carolyn Colleen

What I love to do with the next generation of leaders is to really honor what they bring to the table. It's not necessarily how many years you have under your belt. It's what you bring to the table. There are so many brilliant hearts and ideas. Being able to honor those, give space for them to be seen and heard, and give them that opportunity, just like a canvas, to create.

This next group of leaders has a particular gift in identifying who they love to serve, and why. Once you can get under the why, of why they're serving, that's really where it does ignite. There's a concept of, when the why has heart, the how gets legs. And so, backing out of just figuring out the how, how, how, how, how—and the who, who, who, who, who—and really getting underneath the why. Why are you? What is the motivator behind serving? And once you're able to get under that, that's where a lot of the magic happens.

Aaron Rasch

How do you influence people? You model it. Young kids love nature. It's the most freeing place to be. So, you bring them out there early. Shape people's ideas of what kind of connections could happen, that they care about. Start articulating a little bit clearer too, with how it feels to be in a group that shares the same kind of purpose together.

When you're in a moment, when you're working together, just inquire about what they like about it. This helps them gain some better, deeper understanding. "Oh yeah. I do like this. I didn't think I like work." But it became fun. And so, these moments, you can inquire with a gentle inquiry and help them notice that these times are fun.

These are cool opportunities to connect. There's a curiosity that kids love. . . . They love authentic joy. When you're able to express that and able to model it, they're drawn to you. And I'm just so appreciative of that. I have the opportunity to engage in thirty kids out of having my one daughter. I got involved in a family. Now, she has twenty-nine cousins. It's a huge Italian family. And it's opened my eyes to the ideas of connection. I connect with some kids more easily than my daughter; being okay with that. Just because you're a parent doesn't mean you're going to be the most influential person in the kid's life, but just be open about how different that looks.

PRESENT
*Living with Intention as We Walk
(What We Are Doing)*

What is your personal purpose here on this earth?

What are your deepest held values?

*In between our roots (past) and fruits (future) is the tree;
the tree of our life (present). The daily choices we make
on how we use our gifts in this world, and the values
and direction those choices are rooted in. Some describe
this as a mission, a purpose; some don't get hung up on
labels in favor of focusing on the act of living.*

> *"We are what we repeatedly do: Excellence, then,
> is not an act, but a habit."*
>
> —ARISTOTLE

Sue Rieple Graf

A lot of things changed in the early nineties for me, and I began to truly think for the first time, what am I supposed to be doing? I left my career in banking that I thought was a good fit for ministry at a church. I had a wonderful mentor, Pastor Mark Miller, and my life really began to change. I began to question, "What does God want me to do?" I worked in ministry for a while, then took a job in special education. I learned a lot there about who I was and about being a humble servant from the people that I worked with and the kids.

Then, I felt a strong calling when someone asked about serving the homeless people at the Winter Warming Center, making a meal for fifteen people. I said, "Well, I like to cook. I can do that. No big deal." Took the meal down and saw a lot of people that I knew growing up, now homeless, struggling with addiction, and I just felt the connection. My husband and I did it together. We volunteered at the Warming Center for ten years, and I truly loved it. I felt a passion for serving that particular population, probably, for two reasons. We were homeless for a while as kids. That was number one.

We were doing the Warming Center together when the Franciscan Hospitality House needed a daytime coordinator. The gal that was running it called me and said, "I don't know if you ever thought about a career change, but this would be perfect for you." I felt called. In a nutshell, over the last ten years, I felt God has called me to this mission to help unsheltered people. And so that's what I've done, including now starting the nonprofit WINN, which stands for What I Need Now.

My personal mission is to respond to God's calling for my life and follow the example of Jesus Christ. I live this out by caring for people experiencing homelessness, mental health issues, and addiction issues without judgment or condemnation. It isn't always easy.

Sometimes it is, but sometimes you take a lot of heat for what you do from people that don't understand what you're doing. I've been called an enabler of people, but I believe that everybody deserves to feel loved no matter what. I do that with some simple gestures of kindness and truly care about them, and they know that. Every day I cry. Every day I laugh. I try to give people hope and encouragement and care for them right where they are, literally and emotionally, and every which way, including driving a van out to find them.

Regina Siegel

Continually learning. I feel I will say that to the day I die. I have so much to learn so that I can give the best part of me and to make myself the best I can be so that I can give to others. Listening, learning. The principles for me are integrity: I want to lead each day honestly, and that means being true to myself too. And personally, vulnerability is something I have to work on, so being my true, authentic self. I have endured a lot of racism, hatred, horrible things from the time I was little and where I live now.

Sometimes people don't understand, so I try to take that ignorance and hatred, and understand typically, it has nothing to do with me. These people don't know me. I pray for them and move beyond to use that as an opportunity to teach when I can, and to know when the person is just not at a place where they can understand at that time. I try to be a conduit to bring people together. That's a continual mission I have had, starting from elementary school. I was often the person with my black friends playing here, and my white friends would be playing there. And I felt like, "Why aren't we all playing together?" Sometimes in high school I was looked down upon as, "You're not being true to this group or this group." I never quite understood that.

I grew up the only person of color in an all-white family, because my biological father was African American. So everyone around me was white. I like white people. I also was often drawn to just learning about unique people. The world is really small. I would question, "Why aren't we talking to these people, just because they're a different color, or just because they might not like soccer? Everything else is the same with you guys. So let's talk about it, let's hang out." Now in adulthood when I have the means, ability, and the intellectual capabilities to do so, really trying to have those learning opportunities with people to bring people together is great.

Especially in the last five years or so, there's been a lot of headlines in the light globally, nationally, about the disconnect between law enforcement and people of color. My husband and I are interracially married. He's been in law enforcement for almost thirty years. I'm biracial. Our children are multiethnic children. Our two boys definitely look like African American boys. When our kids turned sixteen, part of teaching them how to drive is not *if* you get pulled over, but *when* you get pulled over, you leave your hands on the steering wheel. You say, "Yes sir, no sir." You make eye contact. You don't move anything. You don't put your hands in your lap. Usually you can just grab your license and registration out of your glove compartment. But people of color, you can't necessarily do that. Instead, it's teaching them to ask, "May I have permission to do this?"

Our oldest son has been stopped, and I have been stopped for reasons that were not made clear. There could have been some profiling involved. My husband and I are still alive and have made choices that were maybe lifesaving, when I feel like any situation where there's a gun could go bad. So, my mission is to bring people together, and especially a focus on when there are other public servants. I know how hard it is to be a police officer, for example. They're here for the greater good, by and large. So how do we bring others who maybe are fearful of law enforcement or don't understand? Because that's where we get a lot of hatred. You don't understand or you're afraid, and so you put up defenses. How do we try to bring those people together cohesively?

My husband and I have spoken locally, regionally, and beyond, because people sometimes need to hear that message in a nonjudgmental way and ask questions. The only hope for our world to heal is one conversation at a time; getting to know our neighbors, instead of judging from afar. Giving back, loving people to the best of our ability, loving ourselves, being curious, and wanting to improve and give back. I think those are the components of my life mission.

Values

My deepest held values are integrity, humility, authenticity, and always being hungry for doing better.
Learning more not just about self-improvement, but
improvement of the world. Authenticity is the one
I struggle with the most. Bringing my full self. A
lot of the barriers to that are because of the racism
I've endured. Going to a store, being followed every
time, no matter who the person was, as if I'm stealing
something. My husband could not even understand
what that looked like. He once came along with me
and watched from afar. "Holy cow, you're totally
right." Seeing things from a different viewpoint, the
way that we are judged—myself and my children—
on the color of our skin, that hurts my husband, and
it hurts us. So bringing my authentic self, I sometimes have to hone that in. In order for my message
to be heard, I sometimes can't share the whole story,
because it will put people off. That's something I'm
continually trying to figure out.

Randy Nelson

Since I first decided that I wanted to become a teacher, it was because I wanted to help kids, which continues to be the most common answer to that obvious teacher interview question today! As a teacher, I did a lot of cutting-edge things in my classroom. But at the end of the day, I realize that it was the relationships that glued everything together then, and it remains the same now. Through human relationships, I can help make a difference in the lives of others.

The story I can tell is when I went to Rochester, from this small rural area in Minnesota, for my second interview. And in that interview, the curriculum director walked me around the administrative center. Just about everyone in this administrative center had their doctorates. There's Dr. So-and-So, and this doctor in mathematics, and this doctor for science, and all these other things. I was pretty intimidated, because I didn't have my doctorate. I had a master's degree.

When finished, she said, "Randy, we're offering you this position. When is it that you could give us your decision?" And I said, "I'm getting some cold feet here. I'm a little overwhelmed, somewhat intimidated, by just the academia in this building, and the people and their titles." And she said, "Oh no, no, no. Hang on one second."

She called the superintendent. We went down to his office, and he said, "Well, explain to me, what are you reluctant about?" And I explained the same thing, and he said to me, "Randy, don't put too much stock into the titles. I have a doctorate. But what you *don't know* about me is that I'm a musician. My doctorate is all about the proper way of fingering on the viola. *That's* my doctorate."

And he said, "I'm not sure how much that doctorate helps me do my job here every day. But what I can tell you is that a doctorate is more about perseverance than anything else. What I'm looking for, and what we're looking for in this district is we want people that when they have an idea, or when they're given a task to do something, their eyes get big, and they look at it and say, 'I can do that.' If that's you, we want you."

I left thinking, "That's me, and we're going to do this." But if that conversation wouldn't have happened, I wouldn't have taken the job. It was a career-defining conversation, and I didn't realize it while it was happening.

As people, we have nurturers along our pathways. We're never done with the nurturing. We're never done supporting each other along the way. When I reflect on my whole journey, every step of the way, my own self-talk was, "You're not worthy of being able to do this, or you're not worthy of having this." But there were people along the way saying, "No, this is something you should do. You should pursue this. You should look at this."

Values

We are human beings who must demonstrate compassion and empathy. It's the glue that holds human beings together in this world. I have learned this from so many people who are great examples. My dad owned a tavern in a small Minnesota community. He was someone who I grew to understand and respect in my later years more than in my younger, more formative years. While I spent most of my childhood fearing the man, I had the opportunity to run the tavern business one summer while my dad was away from the family, working on his own wellness. One of his regular patrons asked to borrow some cash from the till. I said "absolutely not," and he, in turn, pointed to a green metal bin on the back of the bar. I opened it. It was *full* of 3 × 5 notecards with handwritten tabs for people who had borrowed money. Given his tab was up-to-date, and I knew him, I loaned him the money. At a later time, I pulled all of the 3 × 5 cards in that green box, and I noted well over $3,000 of debts when I added them all up. It was then that I realized that my dad was a giving man, and people respected him for that.

Lynn Nelson

I always felt that teaching was my calling. Opportunities to continue in this career (for thirty-five years) always opened up, and I always found people to support my ideas and opportunities I wanted to provide for kids. Most days, I tried to provide for students the experiences they have not already had.

I challenged kids to work through fears or anxieties, and to try something new that would lead to more confidence and pride in themselves. Kids do not get all the same opportunities, so by giving of my time, I had the best chance to impact a child's life. I had a wonderful job because I could be a consistent person in my students' lives for six years. Because of the relationships we had, I continue to remain a person in their life into adulthood.

Values

My deepest values are hard work and believing in people. Hard work was demonstrated and expected. I watched my whole family be hard workers and give back. So I became a hard worker also. I also deeply believe in people and their potential to do great, amazing, wonderful things.

Mike Desmond

I think we're all called to make a difference and help those in need. When asked, "Can you tell anybody 'no?'" I can't. Because if they're in need, the answer is "yes," and then I'll figure a way out later. When people found out that I took five brothers into our house, they asked, "What are you doing? Why? You must be nuts." You know what my answer was? "Because they need me." No one argued with me after that. I tell people, for some reason, the stars have aligned for me, but maybe I've really just made decisions based on what I felt in my heart, not necessarily the logical thing. Every single time, it's led me in the right direction.

Values

What overrides everything is having compassion for people. Too many people in this world are so quick to judge others when we could be compassionate toward them instead. As a leader at work, you can say, "Oh, they're a terrible employee. They're this, they're that." Until you sit with that person, show a little compassion and listen to them, you may find out what's going on in their life and help them get through it. People don't just choose to be bad. These kids that lived in my house, underprivileged kids living on the street at twelve to thirteen years old and often in trouble. I saw goodness in every one of them, tremendous goodness. Undoubt-edly, they made bad decisions, and I called them out on it. But our goal was to just love them unconditionally. They still have contact with me and every conversation ends with, "I love you, Mike." These young people have never felt true love, until now.

That's probably the number one thing we taught them, "Yeah, you are loved." I've always felt this way. You're the Executive Director of the Boys & Girls Club, and you can talk the mission, and you can hire the people to do the mission but if you don't live the mission yourself, you're a phony. What's more import-ant than any words you say, is that you love them.

Joe Gillice

Professionally, I've always wanted to be an entre-preneur. That's been important to me. I never really enjoyed working at a big company early in my career. Again, my father's influence in opening a small, retail hardware store and having worked that and seen what that was like, I absolutely wanted to be an entrepreneur.

Having had the opportunity to co-found Dalton Education and then over the years trying to build a team and build a company, I remember one time someone saying to me, "What kind of culture are you trying to build? What kind of culture do you have here?" I didn't know, and it was a good question. Learning through experience and building a team, you learn pretty quickly what it means to have a good culture and how that impacts the business. In order to build culture, you have to figure out what values are important to you and articulate those values to the people in the organization.

You also figure out that one of the biggest determinants to being successful as a company are your people. When you have wrong people on the team, it's bad culture, they don't uphold the values, and the business doesn't do as well. But when you have the right people and you have the right values, right culture, and good leadership, the company prospers. I've seen that it works at Dalton Education over the years. The number one value for me professionally are people, valuing our people, developing people, and helping our people to be successful.

Any new hire that I've made a job offer to, I've told them, "I take your family's financial well-being personally." And decisions that we make for the direction of the company, you have to consider how this impacts the people in the organization, and is it going to benefit them and create opportunities for them and be rewarding for their family financially? I take that very seriously.

On the personal side, instilling the right values in my kids has been very important to me and my wife. The most important are hard work, making a commitment and following through with the commitment, and doing the absolute best that you can. Most times when I've had conflicts with my children, it's a result of me feeling like they're not embodying one of those values. I can give you a couple of examples.

I've always told my kids, you've got two main responsibilities. One is great grades in school and the second is pick some hobby, whether it's athletics or something else, and devote yourself to it, excel at it.

I don't care what you pick, just invest time in it and work at it and become good. When my daughter was in elementary school, she picked gymnastics. With gymnastics, she practiced ten to fifteen hours a week. My position was always, you don't miss practice ever. You go to practice, you're committed to it.

We're big Florida State fans. My wife and I graduated from Florida State. We have season tickets to Florida State football. I live in Atlanta. We drive down to Tallahassee on a Friday night, go to the game Saturday, come home Sunday. My daughter would have gymnastics practice from say 6:00 to 9:00 on a Friday night. The convenient thing to do for me would've been to pack up and drive down to Tallahassee after school.

But you've got to set a good example and live up to the values that you want your kids to live up to. So we would make sure our daughter went to gymnastics practice until nine, then head down to Tallahassee. Have a value, stick to it, and don't compromise on what's important to you with your family or professionally.

Similarly with my son, when I feel he's skating by in school or sports and putting in the minimum effort, that's when we have a problem.

Now it's interesting to see that my daughter's in her junior year in college and my son's junior year of high school and those values are a part of them. My son goes to the gym on his own, calls up his friends to go practice his sport. My daughter's diligent about getting great grades in college. It's very rewarding to see those values now in them.

I didn't have a tight family growing up. I decided at age eight to not live with my mother and go live with my father. Then he said to me, "I hope you're more successful personally," because there just wasn't a close family relationship with me, him, and my step-mother. I met my wife when we were in high school. We started dating in the second half of our senior year. We were eighteen at the time.

One of the reasons I was attracted to her was because of her family. She had two other sisters, and they had a close family, and it's not something that I had. So a personal mission of mine is to provide a great family experience for my wife and my kids and the extended family.

Jervie Windom

In my youth I sunk into depression and didn't believe that anyone loved me. I didn't believe my life mattered. If you would've met me during that time, I would've said, "I don't believe in God." Although looking back, I was actually disappointed with God. I started reading a lot early in life. In middle school I was studying transcendentalism and reading L. Ron Hubbard, weird stuff for a child in middle school. My teachers remember that time, because I started writing poetry, dark poetry, because I was struggling. Transitioning to high school is when the depression really sat in, and then I attempted suicide a few times.

One particular time I jumped off a bridge. I jumped, and underneath the water was a tree. I fell on that tree and was in so much pain, I thought the tree killed me. When I jumped, I could not see that tree.

There are moments when I'm just relaxing and being thankful. I think about the gift that I have, the breath in my lungs. And how there was once a tree in a forest that God looked at and said, "That tree." I don't know what storm knocked it down, or how it fell under the water, or how the water maneuvered over it to position it right where it was.

But I think about all of the coordination. Maybe a bird bringing the seed, dropping it in the forest wherever it did, or the wind blowing the seed, and it falling in the forest where it did. The tree growing big and strong, and everyone who saw that tree who thought, "Man, that tree's going to be there forever. What a big, strong tree." And then that tree literally falls down into the water, into the river, and it sinks deeper and deeper. And the river flows over it so much that no one will ever see this tree, and this tree is forgotten for all time.

But God's eyes were on that tree. He positioned it in such a way that he knew when I jumped, where I would jump from, and that I needed something to catch me. That blows my mind.

Your life really is not your own. We were put here for a purpose. If we are willing to surrender to that purpose, we could be responsible for doing bigger things than we could ever do on our own. Sometimes we want to be the tree that grows up strong and big to say that we accomplish something, but imagine if you become the tree that lays down and saves someone's life. Adding value, loving, being forgiving, and serving—whatever that means—is to lay down your life, to surrender to God's plan.

I want to be that tree. I want to be that tree for my community, I want to be that tree for my children, I want to be that tree for my grandchildren. I don't care about my life growing big and strong anymore. I want to matter and accomplish what God created me for, which other people may not see, which has to be okay. If you're the tree under water and nobody sees you, it's okay. Maybe you'll catch a jumping soul.

Dave Skogen

I have a gene to serve people. I want to serve and enrich the lives of other people. That's what Dad did. That's what Jim Hunter does. To lead is to serve. Living my dash (that line between birth and death on a tombstone), as opposed to just existing. To serve and enrich the lives of others, live my dash as wisely as I can.

Carolyn Colleen

My personal mission is to smash systemic poverty. There are doors that can be opened, that freed me personally, that I had no idea existed. Once I was able to see there were doors to be opened, and then also have my own self-worth and confidence with which to open those doors, to see what's inside. It was then I was able to see that perhaps there's a difference between being successful and having a purpose.

Sometimes your purpose does not exactly equate to your balance sheet, but perhaps it is what you're called for. Leaning into understanding your purpose, and what that is. Not everyone discovers it early in life, or later in life. And, sometimes you have to work, work, work in order to feed your purpose, and do something that you love.

It's about getting underneath, into the heart and out of the brain, and aligning with what fills your cup and what fills you up. Sometimes that's music, maybe that's art, maybe that's giving back to others.

For me, it is truly helping the "me" when I was struggling. I've gone from Salvation Army to serial entrepreneur. I got intimate about changing my adversity into seeing the advantage in the adversity. As someone who's experienced sexual abuse from men and women throughout my entire childhood, I had to evaluate the definition of what the world had done to me, compared to what lessons could be learned in order to see an opportunity for flipping the script from what happened to me, to what's happening for me.

Crawling my way out of poverty and abuse, how do you, not saying that it's right in any way, but how do you see what the lessons are that can be learned? How can you emerge from that and heal at the same time? When I think back, from patching together food pantry to food pantry, hopping on the bus in order to get to the next food pantry, child and school back-packs in tow—when you figure out how to navigate, you become very resourceful. When you combine resourcefulness with an education, then you look at what that career might be. When you connect the dots, you see that that equates to a strategist. I created a career in strategy.

Identify the lessons of your lifetime to create something that serves you. My mission is to serve and help others, those diamonds in the rough. Help those people who know that there's something more, they're just not quite sure how to get it, or how to open that door, or even see the door. My goal is to add air, and every person has an ember within them, to add that air so that they ignite.

Sometimes you have to borrow the light that another person sees in you until your fierce light ignites. How many times can we think about that over a lifetime, people that have seen something in us? Often, we throw it away. You can't even say thank you, because you're so embarrassed.

There's that piece of humility versus hiding, where sometimes we hide behind humility. But someone sees that in you, and you can borrow what another person sees in you until you lift to the next level of what they saw.

That is what I'm after. Igniting lights in other people. Through doing that as a human race, we can come together and share tools. There's certain tools for buying a house, owning a house, things that are inconceivable to so many. It's not part of their story. However, those are tangible things that many people are used to. What I want to do is take that education and make it available to all. It's the right messenger, and the right message, at the right time.

Through my story and history, perhaps I can open those doors for people to see that their past does not have to determine their future. Perhaps I can help them become financially sustainable and create a life that they deserve. It's not one shoe that fits all. Not everyone goes to college. It's meeting people where they're at and helping them evolve.

Values

Maya Angelou speaks to my core value of equanimity. Despite the chaos in the world, how do you stand strong? How do you stand in your values and stand without being wavered? You can't break a tree that bends. One of the strongest trees is the palm tree, and it just keeps coming back. No matter what comes at you, you stand in that power of who you are and what you believe in, and practice equanimity.

Growing up in an environment with a lot of untreated mental health in my environment and witnessing things that no child should ever witness, I feel it was a gift. The practice of equanimity, mental calmness, composure, and even temper, particularly in adverse situations, in difficult situations. It's a practice.

We could use that in so many spaces, as leaders. Allowing people to be heard, seen without a particular bias of emotion in the space. There's so much change that can happen when people are given space, grace, and feel that they're heard and seen. That is a basis value I feel is powerful and foundational to the other values.

Other values that come with those are giving people kindness and dignity, and altruism: the concern for others without looking for something in return. And finally, integrity. Do what you're going to say, and say what you're going to do. And, if you're not going to do it, just don't say it. Very simple.

We are evolving as humans continually, every single day. The hope and goal is that you're better than you were yesterday. When you know better, you do better. We all make mistakes. I hope we do. Otherwise you're not learning anything. Giving people dignity when they mess up.

Your friends and family, a lot of times they're so happy with who you *were*. There's no ill will of any kind. It's just that friends and family are *comfortable* with who you were. They're happy to bring up all the things from when you were five, and when you were fifteen, and last week.

But, your mentors, your board of directors, and the people that you seek out, those people are the people that are in love with who you are right now and who you're going to be.

Brian Haefs

It started for me during the Master of Arts in Servant Leadership Program at Viterbo. It's a quote attributed to

Gandhi, but he never really said it. "Be the change you want to see in the world." When I was working at Trane in the factory, there would be a lot of yelling between supervisors and people on the floor. We'd have morning meetings, and I would assign jobs and give them something to think about. One of the first days I said, "Okay, I got one for you. Who said, 'Be the change you want to see in the world.'"

The next day they came back and said, "The quote is given to Gandhi, but he really never said it." We all started talking more about the quote in the morning meetings. What does it mean? I said, "For me, it means if I want more respect, I have to give more respect." I said it over and over again at Trane, and toward the end, I started living it, because it became apparent that I had influence with people. I think that came through respect.

Aaron Rasch

There were seeds of what I feel was servant leadership, but wasn't actually articulated as that until later. I didn't conceptualize these things as leadership values, but just a good way to do any type of work or service.

Basic values of deep listening, which we take pride in using in essential areas of human need, like county jails or hospitals or homeless shelters.

There's a need for a deeper understanding and listening. As I keep moving on in my career, the frameworks of services and newer developments of programming are all incorporating these values, whether it's trauma-informed care, nonviolent communication, or deeper listening emulated with structures like motivational interviewing.

These are all frameworks with evidence that inform them, based on quality. But really, what it all comes down to are these common values. Connecting through that allows us to have a deeper sense of participation in our communities.

Whether I'm relating to colleagues or people I'm supervising or clients I'm serving, this basic fundamental need to feel understood is what we most care about. Servant leadership is a way to level the hierarchy of authoritative leadership, bringing it into common understanding of what brings us more aligned together. Listening closely is a big part of that, right?

How do you renew your soul?

Cultivating a servant heart is a choice; a choice which we are better able to make when we feel aware and connected. This requires us to understand how to navigate our bodies' ups and downs, to "ride the waves" and practice self-love so we are able to love others.

Sue Rieple Graf

I'm not doing enough and need to be better. I pray a lot and trust the Bible. I trust God when he says he's in charge and I'm not. Sometimes when I'm faced with a difficult situation with one of my homeless friends, I am powerless to do a thing about what they're worried about. So I just have to say over and over, "God, you're in charge. I'm not. I'm asking you for the best outcome for this person. I have no idea how to help him or her."

We also go to a lot of live music, my husband and I do. I try to get enough sleep, start each day fresh, try not to carry over problems, or worry. Worry never changes anything; I try to remember that and focus more on prayer. In the end, everything is out of my control except for what I do and say, and how I make people feel. I make a conscious effort to be positive and encouraging. People who are addicted don't need to be scolded because they relapse. They need to be encouraged to get back up off the ground, get up off the chairs. Sit, stand, walk, move forward, take the next step. If you stumble, you don't need to roll down the hill. And if you do, I'm still there for you.

Regina Siegel

It's hard. As I've gotten older, I've learned the value. Because often I was doing so much, I wouldn't take time to renew, and then I wasn't my best self at home, at work. I was just drained. I've never slept well for as long as I can remember, since elementary school. Some of it is just my brain always thinking. I'm continuously trying to process. So I'm learning things like meditation and being still, learning the value of sleep, learning the value of taking time to just be, and not necessarily having an agenda, which is tough for me. But I've always been a reflective practitioner, looking through and trying to improve.

In some ways that's a way to renew, because I've tried not to make the same mistakes. When our children were young I was just going on fumes, like many of us do from work to home, hoping things are at least okay. Now one of my biggest things in the last five years is focusing on simplicity; trying to live as simple a life as I can. I don't need four closets worth of clothes, rotating them around and not even having a place for all of them and being stressed out about all of these things in storage. That's not important. People don't notice and don't care. Simplifying every piece of my life so I can focus on what's important. Having a capsule wardrobe, or focusing on a few favorite meals. Trying to get rid of the things in the home so it's only filled with things that are renewing or have good memories about people I care about. Many people would say I'm an extrovert, I have to be for work. Certainly as a principal, I had to get out there and talk to people. I'm totally an introvert. I get all of my energy from stillness, quiet, being alone, having that time to recharge.

In this quest for simplification, we downsized about five years ago. We sold our five-bedroom, five-bath house that I was cleaning all the time and never was able to be present, because there was always something to do. We moved to a condo on the river. Every day I feel like I'm in paradise, and it's a retreat every time I come home.

Instead of having this beautiful home where stuff needed to be done all the time, I now have a simple home. Smaller, and just the space we need for the people in our home. Almost every window looks out at the water. No matter where I am in the home, that's my renewal. Steps from my door, I can kayak. I can watch as life cycles occur; as the pelicans come in, as the eagles go and grab fish, as the seagulls are taking the remains. We have a bachelor heron who comes and hangs out on our dock every year. He has some special markings, so we know it's our guy, at least that's what we tell ourselves. Seeing him as he's grown, and just seeing the wonder and splendor of life, that's how I find the greatest renewal.

And surrounding myself with people who are adding to my life, instead of those who are detracting from it. I realized I had to let go of some relationships and pray for them. Letting things gradually change and be open to new chapters all the time is really good for me, as well as knowing when to let go.

Randy Nelson

I am an introvert, so I recharge myself mostly by being alone. But I also have an informal support group of current and previous mentors with whom I maintain contact on an individual and somewhat regular basis. They recharge my batteries with both affirmation and challenges. Finally, I take time to notice things in nature that remind me that God has surrounded us with beautiful things. I find that peaceful and soul-filling.

Lynn Nelson

Being around great people. Good conversation or doing things together.

Mike Desmond

It comes through the people I trust the most. Dave Skogen's one I recharge with. Steve Tanke, my dearest friend. I recharge with him. When we were going through some difficult times in our family, everybody said, "We're worried about you. Are you guys seeing anybody?" I know who to call and who to talk to. People that I trust, people of integrity and good judgment. Most importantly, people who care about people, who I know care about me.

Joe Gillice

I love sports. Every opportunity I had when my kids were growing up, I tried to coach. I absolutely loved that. The time you get to spend with kids at four, five, six up until they're off to their high school or middle school teams, I loved watching them grow up. You have more influence than you probably realize at the time. You have these different phases of your life.

The phase I have been in is growing a business, establishing financial security for my family, and raising my kids with values I want them to have. When I look at the next phase in my life, do I want to give back to the community? If so, what does that look like? Am I concerned about my legacy? If so, what does that look like? How do I best continue to foster a tight family when my kids might decide to move to different parts of the country and begin raising their own families?

I decide what's important to me, but one of the ways that I can see myself recharging is starting all over with coaching in our community. My kids may not be on the teams, but sometimes those are actually the best scenarios, coaches who don't have kids on the team. Think about the question of nurturing the next generation of leaders. While you don't have a lot of time with those kids as you're coaching them, you can instill values about teamwork and trust and success for your teammates as opposed to yourself. Those values translate to everything that they'll do in their lives.

Jervie Windom

Rest and Sabbath are very important. Whenever we're able to rest, we're saying there is no threat. Because I'm such a workaholic, it's one of my greatest acts of obedience. When I don't, it's one of my greatest acts of disobedience. If I truly trust God, knowing that he is sovereign over all things, I know that God does not need me, he *invites* me to be a part of what he's doing.

Sometimes that's how we act. "If we don't do this, how's it going to get done? What makes you think that if you rest, then God can't do something? We can rest because he's God. It is an act of obedience, of trust. It's saying, "There is no threat. I'm going to take the day off and the world will still turn. It will not all fall apart because it does not all depend on me because I am not God." I mean, *God* rested because he is God. How much more so can *we* rest?

To find that space I use a process called twenty-one blocks, which I learned from one of my mentors. There's a way that we flesh out our calendar to twenty-one blocks: seven days a week, morning, midday, and evening, and Sabbath is four consecutive blocks. That process helps ensure we are taking time for renewal, so we can rest and be recharged.

Dave Skogen

I pray, and I've been meditating for three years. I meditate for fifteen minutes in the morning and a few minutes before bed. I pick an audio meditation on a topic: sleep, anger management, any number of things. One meditation asks us to visualize a person who we resist, and they know it. You've resisted them for years, perhaps. Visualize them, and visualize ending that experience. You visualize a light in your chest, in your body, and then you portray it out to this person who you are visualizing. Meditation has really rewired my brain.

I do a lot of praying, which is something I seldom did years ago. Steve Jobs said, "We don't know if we're going to wake up tomorrow morning." None of us does. If we do wake up, we don't know if we're going to go to sleep tonight. All of a sudden, somebody you just had supper with a week ago has terminal cancer. He's got two to three months to live. Or somebody had a heart attack and you didn't get the chance to say good-bye to them.

Carolyn Colleen

An intentional, daily routine. Every day, practicing a morning routine and an evening routine to cultivate equanimity and calm. Filling up my cup in the morning and having that space for myself to intentionally plan out the day, the week, and how I'm going to show up. Setting my intentions for the day in my morning routine.

I have an evening routine, and within that practice, I make space for silence. Space for affirmations, visualization, exercise, and reading. I reflect back on my day—what went well and what could have gone better, giving myself grace.

There's also an element of forgiveness for the things that didn't get done and setting it up for what's next. How am I thinking, being grateful for the day, what my values are, my family, and setting it up for the next day. Each day, intentionally setting that time aside for a morning and an evening practice.

Brian Haefs

I need nature. It can be as simple as, we have bird feeders in our backyard we can see from our windows. My wife comes from a farm family, and we go there at least once a month, just to be in nature. It seems to ground me.

I go deer hunting every year, and I don't shoot. I carry a gun, but I don't shoot. It's something about nature, being around something wild, but yet you're not part of it. We get to observe, and if we're lucky, see something wild. That's something that we've lost in ourselves, that wildness, that edge.

I don't want to take life. I like being around my brothers-in-law. And a lot of times I'll get out there and get cold, and it might be 10:00 in the morning. I'll go back in and drink coffee with my mother-in-law. It doesn't matter. Maybe it isn't *just* nature. Maybe it's being around people you love.

Aaron Rasch

I would feel a lot more depleted if I didn't feel useful. I feel people have a lot of self-created anxieties and drama. For whatever reason, we set up more challenges for ourselves than we need to.

I respectfully challenge that notion that being in the fray of human challenges is what depletes somebody and that we should try to avoid problems. I feel the ability to transcend suffering with the ideology of my faith and the transcendent means just to breathe through it, to be present with it. You have to experience it. I don't think you can do it from afar.

My favorite virtue is openness. When I'm involved in the stresses of life with other people, it pushes me to be very open, in the now and present. It's almost a meditative practice to be very open, listen, be present with people. It has become a habit in my own life. And it has helped me overcome a lot of challenges.

Now, I know people are like, "Openness, is that a virtue?" In my opinion it is, because it leads into awareness. It leads into this idea of presence. If you're not going to be present and enjoy this moment and be available for a living spirit, I feel you're missing a lot.

A lot of philosophies and faiths are missed if you're not present. Openness is the doorway toward the present moment and awareness. I solidify that practice by putting myself in moments with individuals every day.

What is the most important task of a servant leader?

In Servant as Leader, *Robert Greenleaf shared the characteristics of servant leaders. It is important for each era to challenge and expand upon the core tenets required of our collective call today. With the conditions of our world as they presently are, what role do servant leaders play, and what does that look like?*

Sue Rieple Graf

Leaders should lift others up and work for the greater good; for humanity. The most important task for the servant leader is to be humble, kind, and listen to understand people. The best leaders ask a lot of questions and seek to understand the people they're trying to help, rather than being large and in charge.

The main thing I have done is try to build relationships with people. I'm asked, "How come that works so well for you?" It's because I know everybody. I know their issues. By listening to them tell me their problems, and eventually their stories, we've built a level of trust that they allow me into their lives to help care for them and help, eventually, make some goals and move forward. Not everybody. Some people I'm just going to love and care for until they die. I have, until they overdose, or something else happens, and that's incredibly hard. But again, God's in charge; I am not.

The hardest part is to see someone not able to move forward from their addiction. Even if I could lock them up in my basement, I can't make anybody else do anything. I can only be the best me I can be. Kindness, compassion, and empathy, those are the three most important qualities of a servant leader.

Regina Siegel

It depends on the servant leader. To me, it's finding out what your gifts and talents are and maximizing them in the right profession. When you know you're passionate about it, you're good at it. You find joy in it, and it often doesn't feel like work.

For some people, serving and leading might be designing these ornate parties where people can get together, or those less fortunate could have these experiences. That's not a gift of mine, so I think it's finding what your gifts and talents are, maximizing those, and giving them freely and without hesitation.

This changes for me based on my stage in life and learning more about myself: what I thought I was good at, but really I stink at it.

For me right now, it's connectedness. Trying to find mutual connection and shared vision in making the world smaller, so people understand we really aren't that far away from each other, even if we're on opposite sides of the globe or grew up in completely different familial situations, or look nothing like each other; finding that shared mission and vision. I like to say, I'm a connector of people. I have people that have gotten married, are working for someone else, are professionally or personally connected, and it brings me great joy.

Randy Nelson

The most important task is to help others become servant leaders. It's essential to help people understand the fundamental difference between managing and leading; understand the importance of balancing executive decision-making with an emphasis on both policies or outcomes, and people.

Lynn Nelson

To inspire others, no matter what age, to become servant leaders. Servant leaders have to be a constant in people's lives. The relationship has to be built, and then servant leaders have to always demonstrate whatever they are working on. It's for us, WE. The common good.

Mike Desmond

Building relationships and trust. It's amazing what you can do if you do that first and worry about the task second. Servant leadership is about people, not tasks. That's why servant leaders make such great leaders because they are concerned about people. And people know they care about them. You wonder how people get people to run through a wall for them, because they know they're cared for by that leader. I think it's that simple.

Joe Gillice

You can't just say the words; you have to prove it through your actions when working with people. Earning their trust, truly believing they are the most important element of success in the business, and going out of your way to invest time in them are all important.

Once we wanted to see what kind of return we were earning on our investment into pay-per-click advertising. We were spending a fair amount of marketing budget on it. We decided to turn it off for a month to see what happened. Sure enough, the leads tanked, sales went down, and the sales team was negatively impacted because of our experiment.

So we compensated the sales team and paid a commission as if we had maintained our same level of sales and not run this experiment. They shouldn't be impacted financially because of something that I wanted to learn. That went a long way to building trust with the sales team the next time we want to try something.

We all want the company to grow, we all want sales to grow. If this direction doesn't work, then we'll change. It's interesting how at sales meetings now, when we have these conversations about making changes in direction and there are different opinions being voiced. Sometimes we get to a point where I say, "Look, just trust me," and it's almost instant buy-in. That's because I've demonstrated in the past that they can trust me.

It's also rewarding. We have a corporate communication and leadership coach that some of our leaders speak with. One of my long-term employees shared some feedback about me with our coach, which was, "Joe does what he says he's going to do, and he's one of very few people I work with that actually follows through when they say they're going to do something."

There are so many elements that go into your credibility: follow-through, the commitments that you make. They all go back to building trust in your organization.

Jervie Windom

I'm so thankful for Viterbo University; for the examples of servant leadership that are walking around that campus. People that value and love people. One of my sons is in his third year of medical school and did a semester at Viterbo; it changed his life. There's something to be said about being in a place where people see you. And when I say see you, I mean see your worth, your potential; people that are hopeful, people that inspire.

Viterbo is a place of inspiration, and it's the human hearts that are walking around that campus breathing in inspiration, as God is breathing in them and they're breathing it out upon the other human hearts they have been fortunate enough to serve.

Dave Skogen

1. Willingness to put others' needs before your own.
2. Raise up people around you. To make them better than when they came.
3. Understand that servant leadership is work, and something you need to practice.

4. There's no pixie dust. There's no quick fix.

5. Staying humble. Having the mindset that you haven't arrived. You're teachable.

6. Having the courage to make unpopular decisions and gut calls.

Carolyn Colleen

Meeting people where they're at. How might we honor where we have been, in order to see exactly where we are, in which to create a foundation into launching where we're headed to? Even within our human race itself, we continually have things to learn from. What if we looked at it from a lens of our best? Within history, where have we shown up at our best, despite the circumstances? Where have we come together as a human race, in which to elevate the things that make us strong, the things that make us resilient, that bring us joy and love?

If we can take that and apply it to our daily, apply it to our organizations, apply it to our communities, despite all the turmoil. The sun always comes out, and after the storm, there's a rainbow. So how might we, yes, *honor* the difficult pieces, because they are real, and we need to honor them. We also need to take a look at how *might* we, rather than how *can't* we.

As leaders, challenging our perspective, because when we change the way we look at things, the things we look at change. As leaders, looking into those people that we serve, seeing the resilience, seeing the strength, honoring that, and cultivating it, we have an opportunity to evolve as a community to uplift those strengths and appreciate. What you appreciate appreciates. How do we appreciate where we've been, in order to create a strong foundation for who launches into the next, or where we're headed?

Within servant leadership, it's the practice of not focusing on the problem, but focusing on what's right.

Brian Haefs

When I was a senior and captain of my high school football team, one of the seniors was caught drinking. It was the athletic director's son. The coach came to the team and said, "This guy made a mistake. He knows it. So I want to take a vote to see if he gets to stay or not." We voted, and it was a tie, and the coaches decided we were going to let him stay on the team.

I thought, "Well, that's not how I voted, but okay." Another player came to me and said, "You're the captain. I don't like the way that turned out. I think that's wrong. You have to do something about it." I said I'd be happy to do whatever needs to be done, if it will bring us closer together. So let's talk about what needs to be done and how it'll bring us closer together. And we did that for about fifteen minutes, and we couldn't come up with anything. It was just going to divide us. Looking back, that's what servant leadership's about. Bringing people together, finding common ground.

Servant leadership is something people talk about, but don't embrace a lot, because you're giving so much of yourself. And it's a journey. You have to really be called.

Aaron Rasch

We don't trust each other enough. We've had more trust than we had fifty years ago. When a community doesn't trust, it's not willing to open up to those vulnerable connections. Trust is a value.

We can be led by innovative and collaborative ideas. But they're really value-driven. When we have groups that can trust each other, they will lead us into new areas of development. That's where servant leadership plays a role.

We have to start cultivating organizations that are driven with values. We have to start looking at how organizations can collaborate with each other. They will do that on shared values, because they can trust they will both help each other.

Terms

Leadership

"We need more women in leadership roles, so they can pave the way for other women." It was the spark that lit my flame. In Dr. Jodi Vandenberg-Daves's classroom inside Wimberly Hall on the University of Wisconsin–La Crosse campus, it was 2009, and our class full of young women hovered on the edge of our adult lives. In that cocoon with only glimpses of the real world that awaited us, Dr. Vandenberg-Daves spoke those words. And I determined, as many of us did that semester, that I would do that work. I would lead to serve the generations behind me.

Merriam-Webster defines "lead" as "to guide on or along the way" in both the transitive and intransitive sense; meaning it can have a direct object (she leads him), or it can be a general state (she leads).[8] In the latter, the object is implied or may be imagined; in the former, it is specifically identified.

"Lead" derives from the Old English "lædan," a transition verb meaning "to guide; cause to go with oneself; march at the head of, go before as a guide, accompany and show the way; carry on; sprout forth, bring forth; pass (one's life)."

Estimated dates of Old English usage are 450–1150. The intransitive meaning of "lead," blurring the object from the equation and transforming the verb into a more intangible concept, appeared in the 1570s.[9]

Greenleaf speculated, "I suspect that we will never have a firm, scientifically rooted definition of leadership. Man is an evolving creature, and societies in all their relationships are evolving; and this evolutionary development is far from finished. Furthermore, what is takes to lead will also continue to evolve."[10]

I don't recall the exact moment, but after I left my collegiate cocoon in 2010, my own interpretation of leading became intransitive. It happened sometime after a boss told me I'd someday have her job as the head of communications for an S&P 500 company, and sometime before a job interview a year later when I stated my goals as, "I want to be in the C-suite."

Leading became more about serving my ego or fighting an imagined perpetrator in my path to victory than the lives of the people I aspired to help in that university classroom. Leading was about the leader, not the led.

Interestingly, the emergence of the intransitive form of the verb occurred sometime during the beginnings of modern colonialism. The past five hundred years have created a lot of baggage around leadership, as modern history's more notorious leaders include authoritarian figures who have led with patriarchal principles and perpetrated mass injustices against humanity.

The de-objectification of the act of leadership, the separation of its action from its object—another human soul—just so happened to directly precede the emergence of "lead" as conceptual, detached, and intransitive.

Whether correlation or causation, it's worth reflecting on the sentiment attributed to Rabbi Abraham Joshua Heschel, "words create worlds."[11]

Leading to me at twenty-five years old had turned into a game. It was about being the best, the most perfect, the most likable, the most productive. It was a game I was determined to win, simply because it spiked my dopamine.

My experience with the distortion of leadership is certainly not unique. Capitalist systems perpetuate competition and reward winners. Many businesses pay more money to people who make them more money. Many businesses still use individual performance as the rubric for promoting people into leadership roles, over collaboration, sustainability, and care for the whole.

Servant leadership, therefore, could be considered a radical reclamation and healing of a word.

But what if we refused to let the past five hundred years of baggage and our present systems block our forward view?

Without denying their existence—egoic derivatives, injustices, perpetrators, and victims—what if we accepted the past and present for what they are and moved forward with resolution and a heart full of love for a better future?

What would *that* leadership look like? It would be difficult, and what society would it create?

One where more women are in leadership roles? One where the least privileged benefit? Writer and emergent strategist adrienne maree brown issues a call that our next term stands ready to answer: "It is time to move towards ways of being that are focused on listening to each other deeply and accepting each other, whole. We need to learn ways of being in space together that help us see beyond false constructs of superiority and inferiority without asking us to sacrifice what has shaped us. We need to study being receptive and nonjudgmental with each other, letting the community hold us until we remember we already belong."[12]

Servant Leadership

Greenleaf, acknowledging the injustices and hypocrisies of our human society, encourages us to think about the problem of where our new seeds will come from and who the gardeners to tend them will be. Rather than retreat from or destroy society, make the hard choice of walking the life of affirmative builders of a better society.

Greenleaf attached "servant" to "leadership" after intuitive insight that came to him after reading Hesse's novel. The main character, Leo, a humble servant who compassionately tended after a group of travelers with food, song, and care that sustained them, turned out to be the leader of a great order that had chartered the travelers' quest.

"The great leader is seen as servant first, and that simple fact is the key to his greatness," says Greenleaf. "The servant-leader is servant first—as Leo was portrayed. It begins with the natural feeling that one wants to serve, to serve first. Then the conscious choice brings one to aspire to lead."[13]

For me, servant leadership restores a word and concept back to relationships. It puts the focus back to the transitive state: the connection between the guide and the guided. This starts with our relationship with ourselves (the portion of the etymology that refers to "cause to go with oneself").

And where is it exactly that we are leading ourselves?

Wherever it is, we are leading others there, too. Conscious understanding of our best guess at a vision, and a direction toward that vision.

Servant leadership compels us to know who we lead. The inward journey compels us to know where we lead. From intransitive to transitive to directive.

Inward Journey

Greenleaf published his best-selling book *Servant Leadership* in 1977. Greenleaf's book was a series of essays, the first he wrote in 1970, four years after an early retirement from AT&T, where he had spent thirty-eight years ascending the leadership ranks. *Servant Leadership* introduced the theory to the world. His final essay in the book, "An Inward Journey," is Greenleaf's spiritual reflection on the 1946 Robert Frost poem, "Directive." Frost and Greenleaf were acquaintances. In fact, Greenleaf once asked

Frost for the meaning of "Directive". Frost simply responded: "Read it and read it and read it, and it means what it says to you."[14]

Greenleaf's essay is a culmination of Frost's directive on how to decipher "Directive." Greenleaf calls the poem "a dependable guide for the inward journey." In the last two sentences of his essay presenting his interpretation, he concludes with: "I submit this as a hopeful hypothesis at a time when hope is dim. I will bet my life upon it."[15]

What is this concept of the inward journey that Greenleaf and Frost describe?

To define it, we must start with the concept of inward. What is inner life, as opposed to outer life, and is there a delineation between the two? Many may interpret the inner life as the world in which psychologists, psychiatrists, and other mental health professionals explore every day.

David Brooks, American cultural commentator, describes the most pivotal point of his 2019 *New York Times* bestseller, *The Second Mountain: The Quest for a Moral Life*, as this: "On the surface of our lives most of us build the hard shell. It is built to cover fear and insecurity and win approval and success." This is the outer life. He continues to then describe the inner life: "When you get down to the core of yourself, you find a different, more primeval country, and in it a deep yearning to care and connect. You could call this deep core of yourself the pleroma, or substrate. It is where your heart and soul reside."[16]

Parker Palmer—author, educator, and activist—similarly describes this separation between inner and outer self. "Afraid that our inner light will be extinguished or our inner darkness exposed, we hide our true identities from each other. In the process, we become separated from our own souls. We end up living divided lives, so far removed from the truth we hold within."[17]

Whether called the heart, the soul, or consciousness, this core inner self that Brooks, Palmer, and others speak of transforms over our lifespan, influencing the decisions we make that show up in our outer life.

Brooks speaks to something we intuitively know and experience: "One doesn't really notice it [inner transformation] day by day, but when I look back at who I was five years ago it's kind of amazing, as I bet it is for you in your journey. It's a change in the quality of awareness. It's a gradual process of acquiring a new body of knowledge that slowly, slowly gets stored in the center of your being."

Brooks goes on to reference the writings of Cynthia Bourgeault—mystic, Episcopal priest, and writer—who says: "The Kingdom of Heaven is not a place you go to; it's a place you come from. It's a transformed way of looking at the world, which comes about when you move more deeply into God and God moves more deeply into you."[18]

The apostle Paul writes of the nature of the journey in Romans 12:2: "Do not conform any longer to the pattern of this world, but be transformed by the renewing of your mind."[19]

Here is where we move from inner life to the inner journey, specifically with the introduction of movement. Similar to Bourgeault's connection to awareness, Greenleaf defines the inward journey as "a continually evolving awareness . . . unique and personal for each reader."[20] Sharon Blackie—writer and teacher of psychology, mythology, and ecology—speaks of the inward journey from a feminist vantage point as "a pilgrimage . . . a search for knowledge, a search for becoming."[21]

Blackie, Brooks, Bourgeault, the apostle Paul, and Greenleaf seem to say the inward journey is the change of our inner life: the growth of our consciousness, our heart, our soul.

Reflection

My biggest takeaway from these conversations with servant leaders is that our work of cultivating a servant heart is a continuous inward journey, united by our three connecting threads of past, present, and future. Not an inward journey because it is done in solitude or private; it is through the influence of, love from, sense-making, and community with others that our embers are stoked to light our way.

"Over many years, I have found more than enough people who want to contribute, to fully engage in solving problems that affect them or that they care about. Or that help relieve the suffering of others. We don't need to motivate them to join with us—we just need to invite them."[22]

In the words of Margaret Wheatley, I invite you to join us as we continue this collective work of taking the inward journey—to cultivate our servant hearts.

Action

"In the end, nothing really counts but love and friendship." It was the last line Greenleaf spoke at a lecture series at Dartmouth Alumni College in 1969.[23]

A little framed placard, no bigger than an index card, sits on our fireplace mantel. It shows the phrase, "Love isn't love until it's given away." It was my grandmother's, and it was the credo by which she lived her life.

To me, a visionary who's always had her head in the clouds, it reminds me to act. I can feel warm inside and tell you "I love you" over and over again, but that doesn't mean you feel it. Love is a personal experience that requires personalized action to stay alive, as Gary Chapman outlined in his 1992 book, *The Five Love Languages*.[24]

We can philosophize and theorize, we can read and we can write, but does what we learn stir our souls enough to act? Can we touch the depth of awareness that allows us to know what information is ours to apply and how to begin applying it? Do we have the resilience to continue the journey between inward and outward life, over and over again?

There is a story about the Chinese bamboo tree. The first four years of the plant's life show no visible growth. But with continued nourishment of the gardener, soil, sun, and water, Chinese bamboo does something remarkable in its fifth year of life. It grows nearly three feet each day—soaring to a height of ninety feet in less than two months: one of the tallest trees in the forest. You see, even though a passerby would never be able to tell during those first four years that Chinese bamboo plant was growing all along, day by day, it was developing a strong, deep root system—a foundation that would tether its eventual aboveground growth.

Like the Chinese bamboo tree, our life's work of cultivating a servant heart is often invisible, requiring intentional repeated action and relationships with others. The continual growth eventually allows us to reach the sun.

Your Inward Journey

Self-Reflection

The Buddhist teacher Chögyam Trungpa said, "Let your wisdom as a human being connect with the power of things as they are."[25]

You have read the responses of other servant leaders reflecting on their life experiences. Each of us holds our own answers to these questions. What journey have you traveled so far? What is it revealing to you? What can it reveal to others? How is it contributing to our collective journey?

We invite you to use the pages that follow to begin or renew your inward journey.

You are on this earth at this time in this life. Reflect on the foundations you were born into and the earliest influences that may have contributed to shaping your consciousness.

Who were your earliest examples of servant leadership, and how did they shape you?

_____

_____

_____

_____

_____

_____

_____

We are on this earth at this time in these lives. Reflect on the arc of time, the collective wisdom that has come before us, and what your intuition tells you about this moment. What you feel in your bones about the role "now" has in the trajectory of the future.

_____

_____

_____

_____

_____

_____

_____

_____

_____

What mission do you believe our era was uniquely called to carry out?

_____

_____

_____

_____

_____

_____

_____

_____

How do you believe we best nurture the next generation?

_____

_____

_____

_____

_____

_____

_____

_____

_____

You are on this earth at this time in this life. Reflect on how you are choosing to live out your days here.

How would you describe your personal mission or purpose here on earth?

_____

_____

_____

_____

_____

_____

_____

_____

_____

_____

_____

_____

What are your deepest held values?

_____

_____

_____

_____

_____

_____

_____

_____

_____

How do you recharge and renew your soul?

_____

_____

_____

_____

_____

_____

_____

_____

What do you believe is the most important task of a

servant leader?

_____

_____

_____

_____

_____

_____

_____

_____

_____

Action Plan

Revisit these questions and answers regularly. We are dynamic and constantly growing.

What is my vision for the ideal state of our world?

_____

_____

_____

_____

_____

_____

_____

_____

What is my vision for the ideal state of my life? (Picture yourself at the end of life. Who are you? What life are you leading? What do you believe? What impact have you had?)

_____

_____

_____

_____

_____

_____

_____

_____

_____

With who I am, what I have, and where I am now, how can I best live out my life vision now? (This answer holds your purpose.)

_____

_____

_____

_____

_____

_____

_____

_____

_____

_____

What values guide the choices that I make, which support the fulfillment of my visions? (These can also be aspirational; values you feel you must consciously work to embody to fulfill your life vision.)

_____

_____

_____

_____

_____

_____

_____

_____

_____

_____

What strategies will I pursue now to move me toward my vision?

_____

_____

_____

_____

_____

_____

_____

_____

_____

_____

_____

_____

_____

_____

_____

_____

Notes

1. Sherri Mitchell, *Sacred Instructions* (Berkeley, CA: North Atlantic Books, 2018), 215–227.

2. Robert Greenleaf, *The Servant as Leader* (Atlanta: The Greenleaf Center for Servant Leadership, 1970, 1991, 2008), 48.

3. See Krista Tippett's notion of "living the questions in a world that is in love with answers" from Rainer Maria Rilke's *Letters to a Young Poet*. "And the point is, to live everything. Live the questions now. Perhaps you will then gradually, without noticing it, live along some distant day into the answer." https://www.nytimes.com/interactive/2022/07/05/magazine/krista-tippett-interview.html.

4. Rick Kyte, "How Will You Spend Your Life?" *La Crosse Tribune*, May 3, 2020. https://lacrossetribune.com/opinion/columnists/richard-kyte-how-will-you-spend-your-life/article_c8395086-7fb8-5970-a5bc-cd16fcde0271.html.

5. James Boggs and Grace Lee Boggs, *Revolution and Evolution* (New York: NYU Press, 1974), 168.

6. Robert Greenleaf, *On Becoming a Servant Leader* (San Francisco: Jossey Bass, 1996), 80.

7. Richard Louv, *The Nature Principle: Human Restoration and the End of Nature-Deficit Disorder* (Chapel Hill, NC: Algonquin Books of Chapel Hill, 2011).

8. Merriam-Webster, s.v. "lead," accessed October 16, 2022, https://www.merriam-webster.com/dictionary/lead.

9. Online Etymology Dictionary, s.v. "lead," accessed October 16, 2022, https://www.etymonline.com/word/lead.

10. Robert Greenleaf, *On Becoming a Servant-Leader* (San Francisco: Jossey-Bass, 1996), 292.

11. Abraham Joshua Heschel, *Moral Grandeur and*

Spiritual Audacity: Essays (New York: Farrar, Straus and Giroux, 1997), viii.

12. adrienne maree brown, *Holding Change: The Way of Emergent Strategy Facilitation and Mediation* (Chico, CA: AK Press, 2021), 9.

13. Robert K. Greenleaf, *Servant Leadership* (Mahwah, NJ: Paulist Press, 1977), 27.

14. Greenleaf, *Servant Leadership*, 329.

15. Greenleaf, *Servant Leadership*, 340.

16. David Brooks, *The Second Mountain: The Quest for a Moral Life* (New York: Random House, 2019), 42.

17. Parker Palmer, *A Hidden Wholeness: The Journey Toward an Undivided Life* (San Francisco: Jossey-Bass, 2014), 4.

18. Brooks, *The Second Mountain*, 251.

19. English Standard Version Bible, 2001, Romans 12:2.

20. Greenleaf, *Servant Leadership*, 340.

21. Sharon Blackie, *If Women Rose Rooted* (Tewkesbury, UK: September Publishing, 2017), 97.

22. Margaret Wheatley, *Who Do We Choose to Be?*

(Oakland, CA: Berrett-Koehler Publishers, Inc., 2017), 270.

23. Greenleaf, *On Becoming a Servant Leader*, 338.

24. Gary Chapman, *The Five Love Languages* (Chicago: Northfield Publishing, 1992).

25. Carolyn Rose Gimian, *The Collected Works of Chögyam Trungpa,* Vol. 9 (Boulder, CO: Shambhala, 2017), 328.

Bibliography

Blackie, Sharon. *If Women Rose Rooted* (Tewkesbury, UK: September Publishing, 2017).

Boggs, James and Grace Lee. *Revolution and Evolution* (New York: NYU Press, 1974).

Brooks, David. *The Second Mountain: The Quest for a Moral Life* (New York: Random House, 2019).

brown, adrienne maree. *Holding Change: The Way of Emergent Strategy Facilitation and Mediation* (Chico, CA: AK Press, 2021).

English Standard Version Bible, 2001.

Gimian, Carolyn Rose. *The Collected Works of Chögyam Trungpa*, Vol. 9 (Boulder, CO: Shambhala, 2017).

Greenleaf, Robert. *On Becoming a Servant-Leader*

(San Francisco: Jossey-Bass, 1996).

———. *The Servant as Leader* (Atlanta: The Greenleaf Center for Servant Leadership, 1970, 1991, 2008).

———. *Servant Leadership* (Mahwah, NJ: Paulist Press, 1977).

Heschel, Abraham Joshua. *Moral Grandeur and Spiritual Audacity: Essays* (New York: Farrar, Straus and Giroux, 1997).

Kyte, Rick. "How Will You Spend Your Life?" *La Crosse Tribune*, May 3, 2020. https://lacrossetribune.com/opinion/columnists/richard-kyte-how-will-you-spend-your-life/article_c8395086-7fb8-5970-a5bc-cd16fcde0271.html.

Louv, Richard. *The Nature Principle: Human Restoration and the End of Nature-Deficit Disorder* (Chapel Hill, NC: Algonquin Books of Chapel Hill, 2011).

Marchese, David. "Krista Tippett Wants You to See All the Hope That's Hidden." *New York Times*, July 7, 2022. https://www.nytimes.com/interactive/2022/07/05/magazine/krista-tippett-interview.html.

Merriam-Webster, s.v. "lead," accessed October 16, 2022. https://www.merriam-webster.com/dictionary/lead.

Mitchell, Sherri. *Sacred Instructions* (Berkeley, CA: North Atlantic Books, 2018).

Online Etymology Dictionary, s.v. "lead," accessed October 16, 2022. https://www.etymonline.com/word/lead.

Palmer, Parker. *A Hidden Wholeness: The Journey Toward an Undivided Life* (San Francisco: Jossey-Bass, 2014).

Wheatley, Margaret. *Who Do We Choose to Be?* (Oakland, CA: Berrett-Koehler Publishers, Inc., 2017).

Biographies

Carolyn Colleen

Carolyn Colleen is a fierce mother of three children, author, international speaker, entrepreneur, and business strategist focused on helping individuals achieve their goals while maintaining a balanced family and lifestyle. Carolyn is the founder of FIERCE Foundation, author of *F.I.E.R.C.E.: Transform Your Life in the Face of Adversity, 5 Minutes at a Time!,* and owner of Acton Academy Midwest. She is also a 2023 delegate for the United Nations Commission on the Status of Women.

Mike Desmond

Mike has been dedicated to the well-being of youth, serving as a teacher and coach at Aquinas Catholic School for twenty-five years and then ten years as executive director of the Boys & Girls Clubs of Greater La Crosse, serving at-risk youth. He also serves as president of the Greater La Crosse Mental Health Coalition, a nonprofit organization dedicated to focusing on youth mental health.

Joe Gillice

Joe Gillice is an executive with more than twenty years of experience in the financial services training industry. In 2005, Mr. Gillice cofounded Dalton Education, a leading provider of innovative financial planning education programs and review for the CFP® certification examination. He served as the president of Dalton Education until 2019. Dalton Education was sold to Leeds Equity in 2017, where it became the platform company that launched CeriFi in 2019. Mr. Gillice is currently the chief operating officer at CeriFi, a leader in financial services education and training.

Brian Haefs

Brian Haefs has been an operations manager with ZF Group and member of the Onalaska School District Board for more than a decade. He is a graduate of Viterbo University's Master of Servant Leadership Program.

Randy and Lynn Nelson

Randy and Lynn Nelson are lifelong educators who met during their first year of teaching at a small rural high school in Minnesota. Lynn, a graduate of Concordia College in Moorhead, completed a master's degree in teaching at Mankato State University. With thirty-five years of teaching experience in K–12 health and physical education, Lynn has built strong, lasting relationships with students and colleagues alike. Randy, who completed his undergraduate experience at Southwest Minnesota State University, completed a master's degree in curriculum and instruction at Mankato State University and an administrative specialist degree at the University of Minnesota. In his thirty-seven-year career, Randy has served in the capacity of teacher, director of curriculum and instruction, and most recently as superintendent of schools in La Crosse, Wisconsin. Both recently retired, Lynn and Randy continue to support the community and stay busy with family and community events.

Aaron Rasch

Aaron Rasch has more than twenty years of experience assisting people with complex challenges related to mental illness, addiction, income insecurity, disabilities, and homelessness, He chaired the La Crosse Mental Health Coalition of Greater La Crosse and cochaired the Wisconsin Recovery Implementation Task Force. He has facilitated more than one hundred classes and workshops related to mental health recovery and peer support. While working at Western Technical College, he assisted hundreds of people, helping them transition from jail and obtain employment. He coordinated and directed a Peer Respite program while coordinating a Catholic Worker house in La Crosse. He holds an MA degree in servant leadership from Viterbo University and currently works at My Choice Wisconsin in Madison, Wisconsin.

Sue Rieple Graf

Sue is a caretaker and advocate for the unsheltered. She is the executive director of WINN (What I Need Now), a nonprofit that provides aid to people experiencing homelessness.

Regina Siegel

Regina Siegel is the vice president of Organizational Development at Trust Point Inc., entering the financial service sector after dedicating more than twenty years of her life to education, administration, and nonprofit work. Regina and her husband, John (sheriff for La Crosse County, Wisconsin), are regularly sought after as speakers and enjoy sharing their personal stories, joys, and challenges of twenty-first century life as a midwestern interracially married couple. The duo recently celebrated their twenty-fifth wedding anniversary and have three adult children, two of whom are in college.

Dave Skogen

Dave Skogen is chairman of Festival Foods, a forty-plus-store regional grocery chain that has implemented servant leadership into their culture. Festival Foods stores span across the state of Wisconsin.

Jervie Windom

Born in Brooklyn, New York, Jervie Lamont Windom honorably served twenty-four years in the US Army. Jervie is an alumnus of Southern Wesleyan University, Villanova University, and Viterbo University. Jervie is married to the lovely Nilda Windom, a native of Neptune, New Jersey. Nilda is a US Army veteran as well, with sixteen years of honorable service.

Other Books in the
Servant Leadership Series

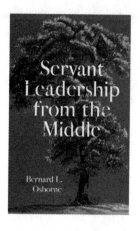

"If you are open-minded, a conceptual thinker, you will find yourself unable to put this book down."

—**Richard R. Pieper, Sr.,**
Robert Greenleaf Center
for Servant Leadership

*Servant Leadership from
the Middle*
by Bernard Osborne
978-1-68275-338-5

Available at
www.
fulcrumbooks.com
or anywhere
books are sold

"A rare, surprising tale of a teenage girl's struggle with adolescence, love of family and country, ethics, humanity, and survival under Nazi occupation of Belgium and France."

—**Peter Feigl,**
retired international business executive, senior Defense Department arms negotiator, and Holocaust lecturer and survivor

*Squirrel Is Alive: A Teenager in
the Belgian Resistance and French
Underground*
by Mary Rostad
978-1-68275-3774

About the Author

Caitlin Mae Lyga Wilson is a mother, writer, and native of La Crosse, Wisconsin. She received her undergraduate degree from the University of Wisconsin–La Crosse and received her master's degree in servant leadership from Viterbo University. She serves as vice president of communications and inclusion at Marine Credit Union and has spent nearly two decades nurturing connections through her work in communications.